YOU!

*

ED YOUNG

YOU!

*

THE JOURNEY *to the* CENTER OF YOUR WORTH

HOWARD
PUBLISHING CO.

OUR PURPOSE AT HOWARD PUBLISHING IS TO:

- *Increase faith* in the hearts of growing Christians
- *Inspire holiness* in the lives of believers
- *Instill hope* in the hearts of struggling people everywhere

BECAUSE HE'S COMING AGAIN!

You! © 2005 Ed Young
All rights reserved. Printed in the United States of America
Published by Howard Publishing Co., Inc.
3117 North Seventh Street, West Monroe, LA 71291-2227
www.howardpublishing.com

05 06 07 08 09 10 11 12 13 14   10 9 8 7 6 5 4 3 2 1

Edited by Between the Lines
Interior design by John Mark Luke Designs
Cover design by Studiogearbox.com

Library of Congress Cataloging-in-Publication Data
Young, Ed, 1961–
    You! : the journey to the center of your worth / Ed Young.
      p. cm.
    ISBN 1-58229-446-1
      1. Self-esteem—Religious aspects—Christianity. I. Title.

  BV4598.24.Y68 2005
  248.4—cd22
                                                            2005046134

Unless otherwise noted, Scripture quotations are taken from the HOLY BIBLE, NEW INTERNATIONAL VERSION ®. Copyright © 1973, 1978, 1984 by International Bible Society. Used by permission of Zondervan Publishing House. All rights reserved.
Scripture quotations marked NLT are taken from the *Holy Bible, New Living Translation*, copyright © 1996. Used by permission of Tyndale House Publishers, Inc., Wheaton, Illinois 60189. All rights reserved. Scripture quotations marked TLB are taken from *The Living Bible*, copyright © 1971. Used by permission of Tyndale House Publishers, Inc., Wheaton, Illinois 60189. All rights reserved. Scripture quotations marked GNT are taken from the GOOD NEWS TRANSLATION, SECOND EDITION. Copyright © 1992 by American Bible Society. Used by permission. All rights reserved. Scripture quotations marked PHILLIPS are taken from The New Testament in Modern English, copyright © 1958, 1960, 1972 by J. B. Phillips. All rights reserved.

Any emphases (in italics) or parenthetical comments within scripture are the author's.

CONTENTS

ACKNOWLEDGMENTS

This is a special book for me because it's based on one of my favorite sermon series over the past fifteen years at Fellowship Church. In that regard, I must thank the people of Fellowship for their constant encouragement to me as their pastor, encouragement that has helped me along the journey to the center of my worth.

I also thank a couple of gentlemen who helped directly in the research, writing, and editing of the manuscript: Cliff McNeely and Andy Boyd. I could not have met the deadline without their able assistance.

And I cannot leave out the good people at Howard Publishing for again allowing me to publish with them. This is my third book with them, and I continue to appreciate the fine work they do.

INTRODUCTION

It's All about You!

INTRODUCTION

It's all about you! You didn't misread that. This book is all about *you*! It's a journey of self-discovery to find out who you are and who you were meant to be. I'm not referring to some ego-driven, self-centered trip. I'm talking about finding the real you, the person God created you to be. Understanding your uniqueness and worth in God's eyes is fundamental to living the kind of meaningful, purpose-packed life God wants for you.

Before we go any further, I realize some readers may have an aversion to anything having to do with self-esteem. You may be one of those. Maybe you were brought up in the anti-self-esteem camp, and this kind of talk about self just doesn't feel right. You're not alone.

Many Christians believe that the concepts of self-esteem and self-worth are unbiblical. In fact, they believe we have no worth at all. As proof, they point out verses like Isaiah 64:6, which says that sin has made us unclean and even our best deeds are no better than filthy rags. Teaching on self-esteem, they further argue, takes the focus off God and puts it on us. We should be promoting not our own worth but rather his worth and his glory.

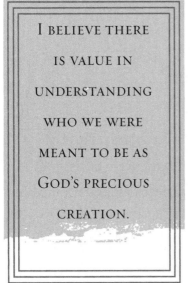

I BELIEVE THERE IS VALUE IN UNDERSTANDING WHO WE WERE MEANT TO BE AS GOD'S PRECIOUS CREATION.

I appreciate the underlying cautions in that argument.

If taught improperly and unbiblically, principles of self-worth can quickly derail into a self-esteem movement that pushes God out of the picture. That's not the kind of attitude we're exploring here.

The reason I'm writing this book is because I believe there is value in understanding who we were meant to be as God's precious creation. Yes, sin has tainted us; it has marred our image. That grim reality, however, must not

4

overshadow the greater reality of our intrinsic worth in God's eyes—a truth evident in the Bible from Creation to Revelation.

With that said, it is my intention in the pages to come to provide a biblical counterpoint to the cultural version of self-esteem that pits vanity against value, wealth against worth, and upward mobility against a higher calling.

When we begin to understand how valuable we are in God's eyes, we can begin to really live the lives God has in store for us. And when we do that, God is glorified.

CHAPTER 1

ME, MYSELF,
AND WHY

When I was forty years old, I realized I had not undergone a complete physical examination by my doctor in over ten years, so I scheduled an appointment. For three hours I was put through a battery of tests that, for the most part, were fairly simple and not overly strenuous. Then I walked into the room where the last test would be conducted.

In the middle of this little room was a mass of wires, cables, and monitoring devices attached to a treadmill. And standing next to the treadmill was a sinister-looking medical technician. He told me to take off my shirt, and then he proceeded to shave some patches of hair off my chest. The next thing I knew, electrodes and wires were stuck strategically all over my torso. A few minutes later, the doctor finally clued me in about what was going to happen. "Ed, we're going to administer a stress test."

The technician told me to get on the treadmill and walk until I couldn't walk anymore. *This is going to be no problem*, I thought. *I work out, I jog—I know I can last two, three, maybe even four hours walking on this thing.*

I got started, and before long the speed and incline of the treadmill increased. Every few minutes the technician would slow it down and decrease the grade, then build them up again. To my horror, the treadmill went faster and steeper each time!

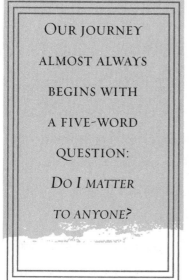

OUR JOURNEY ALMOST ALWAYS BEGINS WITH A FIVE-WORD QUESTION: DO I MATTER TO ANYONE?

After about twenty-five minutes on this torture device, with my tongue hanging out and sweat dripping off my forehead, the technician calmly asked, "Mr. Young, do you feel a little tired, moderately tired, or very tired?"

I gasped for air. "Very . . . tired!" But I was determined to stay on that machine—I was not about to give up.

If we could look with complete realism and candor into the mirror of our lives, many of us would discover that we're on a treadmill at this very moment. I don't mean the kind of treadmill you find at a health club or purchase through an infomercial; I'm not referring to a piece of exercise equipment. Many of us are on a self-esteem treadmill, and we're determined to stay on it even though we seem to be going nowhere fast.

OUR JOURNEY

The moment we're born, we embark on a lifelong search for significance. A quest for dignity. A pursuit of meaning, worth, and esteem. But too often our search leads us nowhere because we conduct it in the wrong places with the wrong intentions—and many die before getting anywhere near their desired destination.

Our journey almost always begins with a five-word question for which we each desperately want an answer: *Do I matter to anyone?* We have an innate hunger in our spirits that pushes us to try to discover whether we matter in life, to find out if our existence is more than futile. But what is the drive behind this hunger? Why do we have this craving for worth and meaning?

11

We find the reason for our search in the first book of the Bible. God created Adam and Eve in his image. Because they were a reflection of God, they were perfect. These two people inhabited the ultimate environment and were living a euphoric existence. They had it made in the shade. Adam and Eve saw who they were in the eyes of God—they didn't look to other sources for their self-worth. And because they looked only to God for their value, they had supreme self-esteem.

God gave Adam and Eve only one restriction in the Garden of Eden: "Adam and Eve, all you've got to think about is worshiping me and doing some yard work. That's it. You can have anything you want except this one tree that I've planted right here in the middle of the garden. Don't touch this tree. Don't eat the fruit of this tree." And as long as they obeyed this single command, God promised Adam and Eve that they would continue their ideal existence for eternity.

Enter Satan. Satan's sole desire is to separate humankind from God. And he used humanity's inferiority to God as the avenue of temptation for Adam and Eve. He lied to them about the reason behind the one restriction God had given them. "Psst—Adam, Eve—the reason

God is telling you not to touch the fruit is that if you touch it, you'll be like him. You can control your own destiny."

So they ate it.

Adam and Eve believed Satan's lie, that they would become like God. They succumbed to the temptation and ate the fruit. And as a result of their failure to obey God, Adam and Eve lost their secure status with him.

We see in Genesis 3 the first instance of people looking away from God and relying on themselves for worth and meaning—and we've seen throughout history the devastating results.

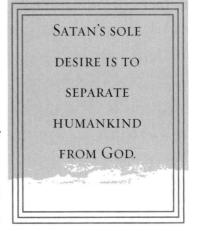

SATAN'S SOLE DESIRE IS TO SEPARATE HUMANKIND FROM GOD.

Since the fall of humankind, we've been struggling with feelings of insecurity and inadequacy. That's why we ask ourselves the question, *Do I matter to anyone?* But as long as we search for the answer outside of God and by relying on ourselves, we will never truly satisfy our hunger for self-worth. We'll never find the answer to that probing question.

TREADMILL HOPPING

People spend their entire lives frustrated, striving, crying, and eventually dying in their search for the answer. But many die without ever discovering the answer because they conduct their search for self-esteem by hopping from one treadmill to another. These treadmills go fast, then slow; up, then down; but ultimately they lead them nowhere.

The Style Treadmill

The first treadmill many of us climb onto in the search for self-esteem is the treadmill of style. We jump on, grasp the railings with white-knuckle pressure, and set out on our trek hoping that style, fashion, and good looks will be the answer. We think, *Surely if I focus on my style and dedicate energy to my appearance, I'll gain the dignity, value, and affirmation I crave.*

The Bible warns us, though, of the temporary fulfillment that comes from this first treadmill: "Charm can be deceptive and beauty doesn't last" (Proverbs 31:30 TLB).

Every time I think of that verse, I remember a joke about two men playing golf at their local country club. While they're getting ready to tee off, an elderly woman streaks across the ninth fairway with nothing on. One golfer turns to his friend and asks, "What was she wearing?" The other golfer says, "I don't know. But whatever it was, it sure needed ironing!"

As tired as that joke is, it illustrates the reality that style and appearance are qualities that erode with the passage of time. The Bible again shows us how insignificant outer beauty is in 1 Samuel 16:7: "Man looks at the outward appearance, but the LORD looks at the heart."

It's amazing, though, what we'll do to make ourselves look good on the outside. Americans spend boatloads of money and major blocks of time focusing on external appearance. Most of the personal health products we purchase are designed to camouflage the aging process.

> WE THINK, *SURELY IF I FOCUS ON MY STYLE AND DEDICATE ENERGY TO MY APPEARANCE, I'LL GAIN THE DIGNITY, VALUE, AND AFFIRMATION I CRAVE.*

Tanning lotions tempt us with that twenty-something, fun-in-the-sun look, and costly antiwrinkle creams promise to turn back the biological clock.

If we're not careful, though, we can become so obsessed with trying to hold on to our fading youthful appearance that we end up trading eternal spiritual rewards for the temporary, worldly satisfaction of physical beauty.

Imagine how freeing it would be to spend half as much time and energy on your appearance as you currently do. What could happen in your life if you used that time to commune with God, dive into his Word, and connect with other brothers and sisters in Christ? Your search for worth would shift from your vanity mirror to the only Mirror that reflects truth and reality.

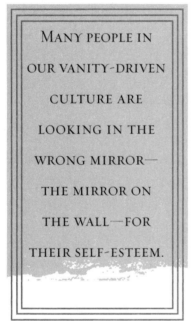

MANY PEOPLE IN OUR VANITY-DRIVEN CULTURE ARE LOOKING IN THE WRONG MIRROR—THE MIRROR ON THE WALL—FOR THEIR SELF-ESTEEM.

Here's how James described the mirror of God's Word: "Anyone who listens to the word but does not do what it says is like a man who looks at his face in a mirror and, after looking at himself, goes away and immediately forgets what he looks like. But the man who looks intently into the perfect law that gives freedom, and continues to do this, not forgetting what he has heard, but doing it—he will be blessed in what he does" (James 1:23–25).

Sadly, many people in our vanity-driven culture are looking in the wrong mirror—the mirror on the wall—for their self-esteem. And they consistently fall short in their search. If we base our worth solely on style and appearance, we're setting ourselves up for insecurity, because they are finite and fleeting.

Am I saying the body isn't important? Are we to walk around with burlap sacks over our heads and never bathe, shave, or use deodorant? Is that what God wants from us?

Not at all.

I'm a staunch advocate of the responsibility we have as Christians to maintain our bodies the best we possibly can. I've devoted entire sermon series to the care of the body, and my wife and I have even developed resources called *Body for God* to help people honor the bodies God has entrusted to them. The Bible calls our bodies the temples of the Holy Spirit. We're to treat them with care and respect. We should try to look as good as possible with what God has given us.

But if appearance becomes our focus instead of spending time with God and serving him, we'll get nowhere in our search for self-worth, and it will wear us out fast.

The Status Treadmill

You may have already come to realize that the style treadmill will get you nowhere. But instead of getting off the treadmill cycle altogether, perhaps you've done what so many others have and jumped to another meaningless treadmill—status.

Status is a great word because you can split it in two and see the true meaning of it. People who are into status

STATUS IS A MOVING TARGET WITH AN ELUSIVE BULL'S-EYE.

keep stats on us. They go through life with a big tally board in their hands, saying, "I'm going to keep score of what everyone has so I can stay one step ahead of them." These people personify the expression "keeping up with the Joneses." And they're convinced that status will bring the answer to the *Do I matter?* question in their own lives.

But Proverbs 11:7 tells us, "Confidence placed in riches comes to nothing" (GNT). You see, the very root of materialism and status seeking is a poor self-esteem. Yet, many of us still believe that confidence can be purchased, that self-worth can be bought. We fail to recognize that status is a moving target with an elusive bull's-eye.

We have difficulty focusing our cross hairs on status because it always changes: "If I can just make a little more money, have that car, wear those clothes, live in that house, move to that neighborhood, . . . then I'll feel good about myself. Then I will have arrived." But what's hot today is not tomorrow. And still many of us continue to fire away, hoping beyond hope that one of our darts will stick, and we will finally find what we've been searching for.

We don't have to look far to see how this plays out in our society.

Consider the people we've chosen as our role models and heroes today. Eager kids and adults follow the lives of professional athletes, pop singers, and movie stars and try to emulate them. Enamored of the fame and riches, they convince themselves that if they could live like that, they'd be happy.

The truth of the matter is that many of our "American idols" are morally, spiritually, and emotionally bankrupt. They've tried the status treadmill, have experienced all the glamour this life has to offer, and found it worthless. Talk to many of them, as I have done, and you'll realize quickly enough that self-worth cannot be bought.

The fame, the riches, the material possessions are not what allow us to "arrive" in God's economy. Those temporal things don't matter to God, and they shouldn't matter to us either. God's warning is clear: "Confidence placed in riches comes to nothing."

The Success Treadmill

After exhausting ourselves on the treadmills of style and status, some of us hop over to the final treadmill, success. We think, OK, *that'll do it. Style didn't do it; status didn't work; surely the success track will lead to self-worth.*

But Jeremiah 9:23–24 tells us differently: "The LORD says, 'The wise should not boast of their wisdom, nor the strong of their strength, nor the rich of their wealth. If any want to boast, they should boast that they know and understand me'" (GNT).

How convicting is that? We're not to boast about the big three in American success values: wisdom, strength, and wealth. Yet we're taught to compete and compare in all three of these areas. We're raised to brag about academic achievement, athletic prowess, and financial gain. Further, we associate these worldly virtues with good old American-style self-esteem.

Despite our best efforts, this success treadmill, like the other two, only leads us to disappointment and frustration. Still, many of us pursue the performance track. We think, *If only I can perform at a high-enough level, if I can do enough to gain the applause or admiration of the men and women around me, that will give my life meaning. That must be the answer.*

I've talked to too many people in these situations, and I've seen it in my own life as well. That does not do it. People put everything into getting on the cheer-

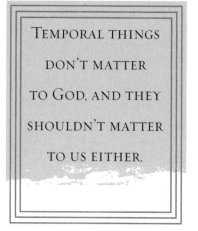

TEMPORAL THINGS DON'T MATTER TO GOD, AND THEY SHOULDN'T MATTER TO US EITHER.

leading squad, working their way to the top of the corporate ladder, making the dean's list, wearing a Super Bowl ring, becoming a major player in the political realm. They spend every ounce of time and energy on these earthly goals, convinced that once they achieve them, they'll finally obtain the self-esteem and confidence they so desperately want.

But when they reach the pinnacle of what they thought would be success, the sense of self-worth they longed for is conspicuously absent. And the reason is that their goals were centered on what other people thought rather than on what God thinks.

Again, God penetrates to the heart of the matter in Luke 16:15: "The things that are considered of great value by people are worth nothing in God's sight" (GNT). Success is just a Band-Aid we apply to cover a deep, gaping wound—the hole that is our need for something beyond what this world has to offer.

"It Wasn't Nothin'"

Sportswriter Gary Smith once interviewed boxing legend Muhammad Ali. The interview was conducted at the fighter's farmhouse, and during their time together, Ali took Smith on a tour of his estate. When he was led into the barn, the writer saw all of Muhammad Ali's trophies, ribbons, and awards on a shelf collecting dust—some of them even spattered with pigeon droppings.

As they surveyed all the boxing memorabilia getting ruined, Muhammad Ali said something very quietly to Smith. He spoke so softly, in fact, that the writer had to ask him to repeat what he had said.

With his lips barely moving, the words seemed to

come from the back of the champ's throat: "I had the world and it wasn't nothin'."[1]

One of the most successful individuals by worldly standards had realized that out of all his accomplishments, none of them contributed to his true self-worth.

Incessant treadmill hopping won't lead to the answer we're seeking, but be assured that the search for meaning itself is not in vain. God wants us to have security, to feel loved, and to find a healthy self-esteem. We'll see in the pages to come exactly who we are in the eyes of a God who loves us beyond measure and who wants the very best for our lives.

CHAPTER 2

TREAD-MILITANT

Stop the machine! Stop the machine!" About thirty minutes after the technician in the doctor's office asked me if I was ready to get off the treadmill, my body nearly shut down. I had finally had enough!

He pushed the stop button, looked at me with a little smirk, and said, "Mr. Young, you did . . . OK." But I honestly didn't care how I did. It was just a relief to finally be off that thing, because it was wearing me out.

Many of us have gone around and around on the treadmills of style, status, and success, but rather than admitting our exhaustion, we've become what I call tread-militant.

We respond to self-esteem stress tests the same way I responded during my physical exam. We tell ourselves,

27

Yeah, I may be exhausted, but I'm not giving up. I'm going to stick with it, even though I may not be getting anywhere right now. Surely it'll pay off in the long run; I'll gain self-esteem if I just hang in there.

We stand firm and assure ourselves that we'll eventually get to where we want to be. We continue to rationalize our treadmill hopping: *Well, that first treadmill didn't work, so I'll move to this other one. Or maybe I'll go back to the first one. Or maybe I can ride two at once—success and style. That should do it.*

But God sees the inevitable result of our nonstop hopping. And because he loves us so much, he wants to show us that we can abandon the relentless treadmills of style, status, and success. He wants us to trust *him* to take the lead in our journey.

STOP!

To stop the treadmill, we simply need to realize the futility of being tread-militant and say to God, "Stop the machine! Turn off the treadmill! I'm ready to get off. I want *you* to lead me on the search for meaning. I want you to be my source of self-esteem." Once we do that, we're prepared to discover that having great self-esteem simply means seeing ourselves the way God sees us—nothing more and nothing less.

God knows that the only way we'll reclaim what was lost in the Garden of Eden is by relying on him, and him alone. Isaiah 49:5 reads, "The LORD gives me honor; he is the source of my strength" (GNT).

When we understand this, when we recognize all we need to do is rely on God for our sense of worth, he will lead us on an ultimate journey of self-discovery. And that quest begins with two simple yet profound truths.

YOU ARE A MASTERPIECE

When God created the universe, he spoke everything into existence—everything, that is, except his most special creation.

When God created Adam, he changed his creative modus operandi. The Bible says that he formed him out of the dust of the ground. And when it came to the woman, Eve, he made her out of one of Adam's ribs. God took personal artistic care in the creation of mankind. Psalm 8:5 says, "You [God] made them inferior only to yourself; you crowned them with glory and honor" (GNT). In other words, each of us is a masterpiece. We are living, breathing pieces of art. God stands before the canvas of our lives, strategically adding color, texture, shadows, and light to make each of us a unique design. And if we let him, if we give him the art supplies—if we give him the brush, the palette, and the paint—he will take your life and mine and turn them into masterpieces.

That should be a revolutionary realization. We are the subject matter of God's artistry. And if we are the subject matter of God's artistry, and God is in the masterpiece-painting business, then that makes us worth something. We are valuable.

One weekend when my wife, Lisa, and I were in seminary, we housesat for a wealthy family. Before they went out of town, they took us on a tour of their home so we could familiarize ourselves with everything. As we descended to the basement, Lisa and I were amazed at what we saw. There, where no one would normally visit, were hundreds of thousands of dollars' worth of collectible art—paintings, drawings, and sculptures. I thought, *Why is all this stuff down here? Why is it not out where it can be seen?*

Is God asking you that very question? Are you keeping his masterpiece hidden away from the eyes of the world?

That's not what he wants. God wants us to share our uniqueness with others.

We shouldn't be hiding in the basement by saying to ourselves, *Well, I'm not really that talented. God doesn't have a great purpose or agenda for my life.*

That's a lie from the Enemy. It's not true. Our lives are made to be on display in God's gallery.

When we clock out and meet the Lord face to face, God is not going to look at you and me and say, "Hey, I wish you would have been more like him or her." He's going to say, "I wish you had been more like *you*." If each of us does not become the unique individual God has created us to be, there will be a hole in history, a gap in God's creative tapestry. Every one of us is an original.

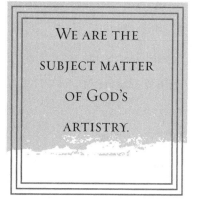

WE ARE THE SUBJECT MATTER OF GOD'S ARTISTRY.

If you had an original painting from one of the most esteemed artists in history, such as Monet or Salvador Dali, would you keep that painting buried in a cellar, covered with cheesecloth? No! You'd hang that painting in the most prominent area of your home so it could be enjoyed by everyone who saw it.

One of the goals of this journey, with God as our guide, is to proudly display our lives as his special creations. We'll no longer want to hide in a cellar. We'll be eager to display our Maker's masterpiece for all to see.

YOU WERE BOUGHT AT A PRICE

Years ago my wife and I had a garage sale. We had gone through our old clothes and old furniture and placed everything out on our driveway for people to pick through. Leisure suits, basketball shoes, torn curtains, and broken toys were strewn across the lawn—stuff I thought no one would ever pay money for. But what amazed me was that it all sold! I learned that people will buy just about anything. I saw firsthand that one man's trash is another man's treasure.

The adage is true, an object is only worth what someone is willing to pay for it. Many times in my life, I've thought, *I don't matter. I'm of no account.* I'm sure you've thought that too. But whenever you begin to doubt your worth, remember the cross—remember the price God paid for you.

That's the second truth you need to know as you take this journey to the center of your worth: you were bought at a price that only Jesus Christ was willing to pay. You are a masterpiece that was purchased at the highest price possible:

"God paid a ransom to save you. . . . He paid for you with the precious life-blood of Christ" (1 Peter 1:18–19 TLB).

In the Garden of Eden, Adam and Eve's canvases were reflections of God. But when the Evil One came on the scene and they gave in to temptation, their reflection was dimmed by the ugliness of sin. And they lost that perfect relationship with the Creator.

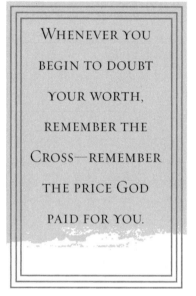

WHENEVER YOU BEGIN TO DOUBT YOUR WORTH, REMEMBER THE CROSS—REMEMBER THE PRICE GOD PAID FOR YOU.

God did something, though. He took the initiative to restore Adam and Eve's relationship with him. Because of their guilt and sin, God took an innocent animal and killed it. They had never seen death before. Everything until that time had been perfect.

Can you imagine their horror at the animal's blood spilling on the soil of that beautiful garden? Can you imagine what was going on in their minds?

God then skinned the animal and used the hide to clothe Adam and Eve, because for the first time, they realized they were naked. They felt the guilt and the pain of it, and the animal skins covered their nakedness.

This is a foreshadowing of what would happen later—the shedding of an innocent third party, the spilling of blood, to cover and atone for the sins of humanity.

Push the fast-forward button. God's people had come under Egyptian bondage. God told them he would supernaturally free them. He also told them that a death angel would pass through the city and take the life of the firstborn of every household. But then he told his people to find an unblemished lamb, kill it, and put some of its blood on the doorposts over their homes. If they did this, the death angel would pass over each household with the blood of the lamb on its doorpost. The entire Old Testament sacrificial system was based on the shed blood of an innocent third party to atone for sin.

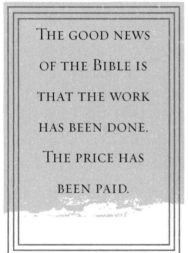

THE GOOD NEWS OF THE BIBLE IS THAT THE WORK HAS BEEN DONE. THE PRICE HAS BEEN PAID.

In the New Testament, we find Jesus living a perfect life. At thirty years of age, he was walking down the street, and John the Baptist said, "Look, the Lamb of God, who takes away the sin of the world!" (John 1:29). He was the ultimate Passover lamb. Three years later, Jesus Christ died on a cross for your sins and mine. Right before he breathed his last breath, he said, "It is finished" (John 19:30). Then, in three days, he burst forth from the grave with resurrection power.

Our sins nailed Jesus to the cross. He took all the guilt, all the pain, all the remorse when he hung there suspended between heaven and earth, taking the licks for our moral foul-ups. He did it because we matter to him. He did it because he wanted us to understand our originality, our value, and to experience his love and forgiveness. The good news of the Bible is that the work has been done. The price has been paid.

That's why the Bible tells us in Romans 5:8, "God has shown us how much he loves us—it was while we were still sinners that Christ died for us!" (GNT). And by paying that price at the cross, Jesus regained for us all we had lost as a result of our sin.

With his atoning sacrifice, he signed God's masterpiece— God's redemptive painting.

Right now, by his grace and by his power, he is saying to us, "Give me your art supplies. I want to do the painting. I'm the artist. I can take your inadequate attempt at finger-painting and make the canvas of your life into something breathtakingly beautiful."

As I think about what God has done for me, I'm reminded of two guiding principles for my life. The first thing my life is about is sharing Jesus Christ with others—hoping and praying they will establish a relationship with him and become followers of Christ.

The second focus of my life is raising the self-esteem of people I come into contact with. So every time I have the opportunity to meet with an individual, a family, or a group of people, my goal is to make them aware of the self-esteem they can have through Jesus Christ and to help nurture their relationship with him.

The most amazing experience for me as a pastor is seeing people accept Christ and become fully devoted followers. When that happens, an incredible phenomenon takes place: the destructive thought patterns, relational problems, fear, disillusionment, and poor self-esteem that were part of their former lives begin to fall away.

That transformation happens because these people finally begin to see themselves through God's eyes. They see that they really are masterpieces and that they were bought with the precious blood of Jesus Christ. And realizing this allows them to finally discover the answer to the existential question, *Do I matter?*

In the rest of this book, we're going to look into what scars our self-esteem, how we can reconstruct a damaged self-image, and how to build self-esteem in others. But the first step in the journey to the center of our worth is understanding this: each of us is a masterpiece created by God and has been bought at the highest price—the precious blood of Jesus.

CHAPTER 3

DAMAGE
ASSESSMENT

✳

Several years ago my family took a driving vacation from Dallas down to the central and south Texas areas. Prior to leaving, Lisa and I had an interesting discussion about all the baggage we were going to take. At the time, our oldest daughter was eight years old, our son was three, and our twin daughters were one. You can imagine all the humidifiers, highchairs, cribs, and diapers we needed to take for an outing like that.

I said, rather pointedly, "Lisa, there is no way we can get all this in one car. We're going to have to take two cars to San Antonio and Houston."

She answered sweetly, "Honey, we can make it in

one car, and I can tell you how we're going to do that in two words."

"And what are those two words?"

"Luggage carriers."

"You mean those Clark Griswold–type contraptions that fit on top of the car that you jam all your suitcases into?"

"Yes," she said. Then she added, "In fact, the auto-parts store is having a special on luggage carriers."

So the next morning, yours truly was down at the auto-parts store picking up two gargantuan luggage carriers. I climbed on top of our Suburban in the boiling Texas summer heat and stuffed all our baggage into the carriers. Finally, with the luggage on top and the humans inside the vehicle, we left.

At the first hotel we checked into in San Antonio, the bellman who helped us with our luggage said, "Folks, I've been working at this hotel for eight years, and this is the most luggage I've ever seen for one family." We stayed there a couple of days and then went on to Houston to visit some family.

When it came time to return to Dallas, I packed everything back in the carriers and made sure they were secure.

We made the long drive home without incident, turned into our neighborhood, and then pulled into the driveway.

I pushed the garage door opener, stepped on the gas pedal, and started to pull into the garage.

Crash!

The enormous clatter was immediately followed by boards falling all around us. To my horror, I realized we had torn off the garage overhang with the luggage carriers. I backed up and got out to assess the damage. Amazingly, the car was OK—but the top of the garage was a splintered mess.

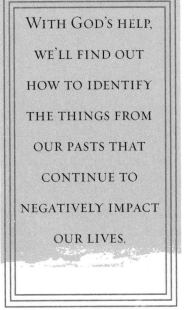

WITH GOD'S HELP, WE'LL FIND OUT HOW TO IDENTIFY THE THINGS FROM OUR PASTS THAT CONTINUE TO NEGATIVELY IMPACT OUR LIVES.

We're all carrying baggage through life. Whether they're carry-on duffels or massive luggage carriers like the ones we took on our vacation, our baggage is packed with words and experiences that have splintered our self-esteem. In this chapter we're going to assess the damage left behind by life's baggage. With God's help, we'll find out how to identify the things from our pasts that continue to negatively impact our lives.

As we cruise through life—as we encounter people at the movie theater, the grocery store, or Home Depot—most of us typically see the same thing. We see a group of fairly confident, attractive, well-groomed, well-mannered, middle-class suburbanites. But under that facade, beneath that layer of apparent confidence and assuredness, lies some damage that's not as obvious as my garage mishap, but far more devastating.

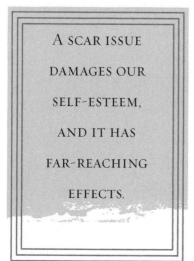

A SCAR ISSUE DAMAGES OUR SELF-ESTEEM, AND IT HAS FAR-REACHING EFFECTS.

Many people are trying to cover up bangs, dents, and broken pieces that are undetectable to the naked eye. To God, however, our damage is obvious.

Each of us has acquired what I call a *scar issue*. You did not misread those words. I'm not referring to scar tissue. Scar tissue is comparatively slight and superficial. A scar issue, on the other hand, damages a foundational aspect of our lives—our self-esteem—and it has far-reaching effects.

All of us have scarred and wounded self-esteem, but

the degree of scarring varies for each person. Some have only a little nick or scrape. Others have severe lacerations, even life-threatening injuries, that impact us deeply. We allow those wounds to cause trauma and drama in our lives for years. Sometimes for the rest of our lives.

But what is it that scars our self-esteem? How do we end up with a damaged view of our own worth and meaning? Scar issue has two basic causes.

The first way our self-esteem is tattered, shattered, and scarred is through the words of others.

WORDS OTHERS SAY TO US

It's not uncommon these days in political and social arenas to hear the cry for gun control. Politicians, citizens, and lobbyists can be heard crying out, "We've got to get guns off the street! They kill, maim, destroy, and handicap thousands of people every year."

Well, as harmful as firearms can be to our physical bodies, the words fired at us by others can have a spiritual and emotional effect more devastating than bullets. And these weapons aren't usually fired randomly, by unknown shooters. The words that cause injury to our self-esteem often come from people we know and trust.

The Bible warns us of the power of negative words.

Proverbs 12:18 says, "Reckless words pierce like a sword." In the book of James, the tongue is likened to a fire, called a "world of evil among the parts of the body" (3:6), and described as a "restless evil, full of deadly poison" (3:8).

James 3:9 gets to the heart of the matter: "With the tongue we praise our Lord and Father, and with it we curse men, who have been made in God's likeness." When we damage others with words, we are, in effect, lashing out against God himself, because we're cursing his masterpieces, people made in his likeness.

From a biological perspective, a tongue is a fleshy, muscular organ attached to the bottom of the mouth. It helps us chew, taste, swallow, and articulate sounds. But a tongue is also a weapon. And with this weapon we can wound people deeply. We can, in a matter of seconds, tear their lives apart.

Thoughtless words spoken by others can wound our confidence more deeply than any sword or bullet can wound our flesh. And while it's painful to think about, we need to deal with some of the verbal junk that continues to mess us up and bog us down.

Take a Step Back

Assessing the damage done to our self-esteem over the years requires a step back in time to identify some of the words that have caused our deepest wounds. In doing so, we'll come face to face in our mind's eye with the people who thoughtlessly hurled these weapons at us during some of the most vulnerable periods in our lives.

As we discovered in chapter 1, the moment we're born, we embark on a journey to answer a question. That question, *Do I matter to any-one?* is one to which we begin to develop an answer early in life.

WE NEED TO DEAL WITH SOME OF THE VERBAL JUNK THAT CONTINUES TO MESS US UP AND BOG US DOWN.

During the critical formative years of child-hood, we establish the foundation on which we build our sense of worth and our confidence. The first people from whom we take our cues on self-esteem are our parents and other childhood authority figures.

If during your childhood you looked to your parents and were lovingly greeted with affirming statements like, "You are loved. We're so glad you're part of this family, be-cause you matter. You are a true gift from God," then you had a great head start in discovering your intrinsic worth.

On the other hand, if you grew up under the glare of

disapproval and were pelted with phrases like, "You were a mistake," "No wonder you don't have any friends," "Can't you just leave me alone?" then the chances are high that your self-esteem was torn to shreds early on.

As we grow, we tend to pile these harmful phrases on top of one another, put them into a shoulder bag, and carry them around with us for the rest of life's journey—particularly the journey to the center of our worth. These words weigh us down and keep us from experiencing the awesome potential we have in God. We haul this extra baggage around because we've never learned how to let it go.

Row, Row, Row Your Boat

When I was in elementary school, something happened that scarred my self-esteem and affected my view of my abilities. For years I carried the memories of that experience with me and allowed it to affect me negatively. In fact, it wasn't until I was about thirty-five years old that I finally was able to repair the damage.

My voice has always been unusually low. I never went through the usual pubescent voice change—my voice never cracked. During the first day of music class in second grade, our teacher had us sing "Row, Row, Row Your

Boat." He detected my low voice and stopped us. "Who is singing so low? Who's joking around?"

Everyone pointed to me, and the teacher was convinced I was playing a joke. So he stood me up in front of the class and said, "If you don't start singing with a normal voice like everyone else, you will go straight to the principal's office." Then he made me sing the rest of the song in front of the entire second grade. Of course all the kids were laughing at me because I didn't sound like they did. It was humiliating.

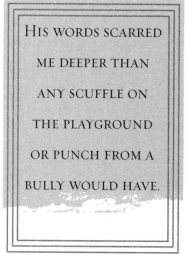

HIS WORDS SCARRED ME DEEPER THAN ANY SCUFFLE ON THE PLAYGROUND OR PUNCH FROM A BULLY WOULD HAVE.

It took many, many years for me to overcome the effects of that moment in my life. His words scarred me deeper than any scuffle on the playground or punch from a bully would have.

Whether in a public humiliation or a private putdown, most of us have gone through at least one similar painful episode. We've been wounded deeply by words from others.

But that's not the only source of damage to our self-esteem.

WORDS WE SAY TO OURSELVES

We're also wounded by the things we tell ourselves. Here's how the destruction occurs. First we hear the lies others tell us—that we're not good enough, that we'll never make it. We hear damaging words that chip away at our self-esteem.

Once those lies infiltrate our minds and hearts, we start to tell ourselves the very same things. Like roasted chickens on a rotisserie grill, we allow the lies to turn over and over in our minds, affecting the way we think about ourselves.

Over time, after hearing the lies repeatedly, we start to believe them.

And the Evil One uses that to keep us from realizing our potential in life. He wants to keep us down and discouraged, and one of the ways he does that is by getting us to believe these lies—that we're less capable, less worthy, just plain less than we really are.

DANGEROUS GAMES WE PLAY

When damaging words others say to us and words we say to ourselves do their dirty work, we play two games to mask our scarred self-esteem.

The Comparison Game

We love to compare what we have with what others have. Our radar constantly scans the horizon, looking for someone or something else with which to compare ourselves. We say to ourselves, *I wonder if he's more successful than I am*, or *She's so thin and fit, it makes me sick!*

Our desire to compare is one reason reality TV shows are so popular. We love to look at what others have and compare ourselves with them. But comparing ourselves with others is a dangerous game that leaves untold damage in its wake.

One of two things will happen to our self-esteem when we play the comparison game, and both of them are detrimental to our emotional health.

The first possible result of comparing ourselves with others is that we'll end up feeling terrible about ourselves. Our self-esteem will plummet. We'll see that someone else lives in a bigger house, drives a nicer car, or has a lower golf handicap than we, and we'll feel bitter because we don't or can't have what that person has. By playing the comparison game, we place more emphasis on material possessions or physical attributes than on what God values as most important—the heart.

The other possibility is that we might book ourselves on an ego trip. We'll compare ourselves with others and say to ourselves, *Well, I'm much more generous,* or *I'm better looking.* What we fail to see when we do this is that we're really calling attention to our own insecurities. It's because we want to soothe our own feelings of inadequacy that we want to know we have more toys or less body fat or more money than someone else.

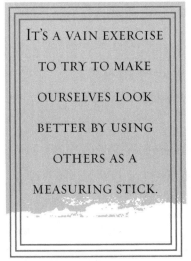

IT'S A VAIN EXERCISE TO TRY TO MAKE OURSELVES LOOK BETTER BY USING OTHERS AS A MEASURING STICK.

The apostle Paul warned how ridiculous it is to make ourselves look good by comparing ourselves with others. He cited the poor example of some in the first-century church who built up their own stature and authority by making such comparisons: "I wouldn't dare say that I am as wonderful as these other men who tell you how important they are! But they are only comparing themselves with each other, and measuring themselves by themselves. What foolishness!" (2 Corinthians 10:12 NLT).

It's a vain exercise to try to make ourselves look better by using others as a measuring stick—looking at what other people do or don't do, have or don't have—rather than looking to God for our worth. Paul concluded his point in verse 17: "'The person who wishes to boast should boast only of what the Lord has done.'"

The bottom line is this: whether we do it to get down on ourselves or to set ourselves up on a pedestal, it's unfair to compare. And it's always a losing game.

The Criticism Game

The second game we play to disguise our own flagging self-esteem is using words to criticize ourselves. Instead of just saying thank you when someone compliments us, we turn those flattering remarks upside down and use them to tear ourselves down.

For example, if someone says to us on the golf course, "Hey, nice shot," instead of saying a simple thank you, we say, "Yeah, it's about time. That's the first good shot I've had all day!" We plant these seeds of criticism in the hope that other people will build us up. We want them to say to us, "Oh, come on! You've hit lots of great shots today!"

When we wear a new outfit to a party and someone compliments us, we respond, "Oh, this old thing?" when we really want to hear again how great it looks on us.

But we take it further than just a golf shot or an outfit.

We want others to recognize our charitable efforts and generosity as well. It makes us feel like we're good people when others see us doing good deeds. Yes, we may give to charity, volunteer at a homeless shelter, or donate our old clothes—and we may genuinely mean well—but deep down we also want recognition from those around us. Then, when we get it, we say, "Oh, but I just wish I could do more," hoping the person will counter with, "But you do so much already!"

Not only do we criticize ourselves, but we also criticize others to give ourselves a shot in the arm. When we see something we disagree with or think is beneath us, we love to point it out. We hope that by criticizing that other person or that other group, we'll look better to the people around us.

But it's a disguise when we criticize. Negative criticism is just an attempt to cover the festering wounds in our own self-esteem. It also makes a mockery of God's creative genius. We're saying that some of his creation is worthy of our admiration while some falls short. It is simply a losing game to do that, because God created each person to be unique.

MOSES'S SCAR ISSUES

Would you believe that the great Hebrew patriarch, the deliverer of God's chosen people—Moses himself—struggled with some major self-esteem issues?

54

Although Moses was born a Hebrew, he was brought up as Egyptian royalty. Some scholars believe he was being groomed to be the next president and CEO of Egypt—the next pharaoh. Moses, though, ended up living in a wilderness as a fugitive for forty years, after killing an Egyptian. When

IT'S A DISGUISE WHEN WE CRITICIZE.

Moses was about eighty years old, God said, "Moses, I want you to be the man to deliver the children of Israel, the Hebrews, out of bondage. You can do it, Moses. I have chosen you."

But Moses had developed a warped sense of worth over his lifetime and told God, "I can't do that! No way. I don't speak very well. I'm not very articulate. I st . . . st . . . stutter. There's got to be someone who can do it better than I—maybe my brother!"

Moses told God that his brother was a better man for the job. He dared to compare himself with someone else.

I suspect that somewhere in Moses's past, people had scarred him. They had wounded him. They had damaged his self-esteem. And the damage took hold and affected him the moment he began to believe those lies and agree with what people said about him.

Maybe the Egyptians he grew up with ridiculed him because the color of his skin was different. Perhaps they laughed at his build or his background. Whoever it was that damaged him, the effects were obvious in Moses's view of his own value.

Moses took in all those hurtful words and carried them around for many years before he finally was able to see who he was in God's eyes and what he was capable of accomplishing.

BAGGAGE INSPECTION

After a fishing trip several years ago, as I was leaving the tiny airport of Tegucigalpa, Honduras, I had to put my luggage on the counter for inspection. One of the officials unzipped my bags, took out everything—and I mean everything—and examined my stuff. He even pulled out my underwear. It was rather embarrassing, and I felt a little violated. But it was necessary before I could start my journey.

If we're going to take this journey to the center of our worth, if we're really going to assess the damage to our self-esteem, we have to let God inspect our baggage. He won't violate us or humiliate us, but he will show us for our own good what in our lives is causing damage.

God already sees everything. Think of it as passing through one of those x-ray scanners before you board a flight. God sees it all; he knows it all. But we can't really trust him until we know that he knows about our problem.

Have you taken that important step of asking God to inspect your baggage and help you assess the damage? Only then will you be able to move forward, rebuilding and restoring the self-esteem he wants you to have.

CHAPTER 4

OPENING UP

✳

So far we've uncovered the tough stuff—we all have damaged or scarred self-esteem. But surely that discovery is not the end of our journey. Certainly there's some way we can redeem our self-worth, recover our self-esteem, and rebuild our confidence.

Is there some kind of spiritual LASIK procedure we can perform to correct our vision and see ourselves the way God does? Well, I believe there is a way, with God's help, to reshape the view we have of ourselves.

We saw in chapter 3 that we can derive our self-esteem from one of three sources—from God, from others, or from ourselves. It's our option; it's our choice. If we choose to build our self-esteem from others or from ourselves, we're choosing a very limited, narrow perspective.

However, as we'll discover in this chapter, if we opt to take our self-esteem cues from God, watch out! Amazing things will start to happen in our lives.

In Hebrews 2:7 we find one of God's self-esteem cues—we find a base for rebuilding our self-worth foundation. This verse tells us that God has crowned us with glory and honor. He has a custom-made crown of supreme self-esteem for each of us.

PAPER CROWNS

When I was growing up, my mother would occasionally take my brothers and me to Burger King. It was one of our favorite restaurants, not only because it was the home of the Whopper, but also because every time we ordered a kid's meal, they would give us one of those paper crowns. And despite the cheapness of those crowns, we thought they were great. We'd put them on and instantly transform ourselves into royalty—at least in our minds.

I have a huge head, so after just a few hours of wearing my crown, it would inevitably break. And being the oldest brother, I thought I had a birthright to the crown, so I would try to take one of my younger brothers' crowns—which resulted in real-life reenactments of the WWF in our living room. The fights that ensued over those flimsy paper crowns were some of the most intense of our childhood.

If we could look through God's eyes into our heart of hearts, many of us would see a huge pile of cheap, flimsy crowns representing the worldly things that have failed to give our lives meaning and purpose. In this chapter, however, we're going to look beyond cheap symbols to the real value God places on our lives.

THE REAL DEAL

Our search for self-esteem is, in reality, a quest to reclaim a real and lasting crown of honor and dignity. We're in constant search-and-rescue mode. But too many of us miss out on the real deal, the crown God has tailor-made for each person, because we waste our lives trying on cheap, flimsy, paper crowns.

We focus on looking good for others, elevating ourselves in the corporate world, or obtaining as much stuff as we possibly can. And we think those crowns, those symbols of style, status, and success, will give us the confidence we so desperately crave. How sad that some of the fiercest fights in life are over those paper crowns.

If we're willing to set aside those paper crowns, though, God will replace them with something real—something of true beauty and significance. Lovingly he whispers, "I don't want you to settle for paper crowns. I want you to have a real crown of glory, honor, and dignity. Look to my love for you, not to what others tell you, to guide you in your journey."

But God's process for rebuilding a damaged self-esteem is not instantaneous or easy. It takes work on our part. Achieving supreme self-esteem is a three-step process: (1) opening up to the truth, (2) asking for help, and (3) diving into God's best. Each step is critical to the next, and we'll walk through each of them together, beginning here and continuing throughout the next two chapters.

OPENING UP TO THE TRUTH

The first step in rebuilding our self-esteem, in uncovering God's supreme, tailor-made crown for each of us, is opening up to him and allowing him to speak truth into our lives. To grasp the kind of self-esteem God wants us to have, in order to have the pain go away—not just be dulled or numbed—we need to turn to God and open up to his truth.

Letting Go of the Fairy Tale

When my son EJ was two years old, he loved Barney the dinosaur. He had videos, stuffed Barneys, and even Barney slippers. Every morning Barney's theme song could be heard echoing throughout our house, either through the television speakers or EJ's little mouth. "I love you, you love me . . ."

If you asked EJ whether or not Barney loved him, he'd respond with an emphatic "Yes!" In his mind, Barney was not fictional; he was real, as tangible as the Cheerios we ate for breakfast.

But as EJ grew, he engaged in some probing conversations with his family and friends. These led to the unhappy discovery that there's no such thing as a giant, purple, talking dinosaur that takes his playmates on trips around the world

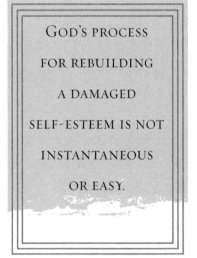

GOD'S PROCESS FOR REBUILDING A DAMAGED SELF-ESTEEM IS NOT INSTANTANEOUS OR EASY.

by simply waving a wand. Eventually the overwhelming evidence demanded that EJ reject the myth and believe the truth—that Barney is not real.

Many of us still believe today the myths and fairy tales we heard as children. We still accept the falsehoods others said about us and to us, and we allow those myths to dictate our adult reality.

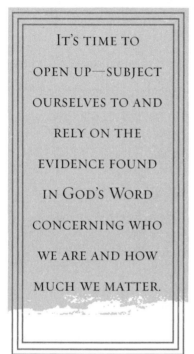

IT'S TIME TO OPEN UP—SUBJECT OURSELVES TO AND RELY ON THE EVIDENCE FOUND IN GOD'S WORD CONCERNING WHO WE ARE AND HOW MUCH WE MATTER.

Imagine how you would react if your best friend walked up to you and said, "Have you read the newest entrepreneurial-enterprise book written by Big Bird? That guy is a genius! I believe so much in his theories that I'm going to base my own business on his Sesame Street philosophy."

After you recovered from your laughing fit, you'd tell your friend to close the storybook, stop taking advice from a fictional character, and open up the book of reality.

We need to do the same thing with our lives. We need to close the fictional books we've been relying on for our self-worth and turn to the book of reality: the Bible. It's time to open up—subject ourselves to and rely on the evidence found in God's Word concerning who we are and how much we matter.

After reviewing the overwhelming evidence of God's love, we'll be able to reject the harmful myths from our past and believe the truth about our condition—that we matter more to God than we could ever fathom.

Discovering How Much We Matter

In Luke 15 Jesus emphasizes our importance. He tells three stories that each revolve around a lost object and the owner's joy once that object is found.

In the first story, a shepherd loses one of his one hundred sheep. After searching for and finding the sheep, the shepherd invites the other shepherds to a party to celebrate.

In the second story, a woman loses one of her ten coins. After tearing the house apart, she finally finds it. Once the lost coin is back in her possession, the woman rejoices.

The third story is one of the most well-known and recognized stories in the Bible—the story of the prodigal son. A son goes to his father and demands his inheritance—he doesn't want to wait until his father's death to claim his birthright. The father gives the son his inheritance. The son then squanders all the money on riotous living and eventually returns home in shame. But the father is not angry. Instead, he hosts a huge celebration. He is overcome with joy because his son has returned.

Through these stories, Jesus is saying that God is like the shepherd, the woman, and the father. And we're like the sheep, the coin, and the son. We matter to him. We are lost, but what rejoicing takes place in heaven when we're found!

If you've confessed your sins, accepted God's forgiveness, and received Jesus Christ into your life, a cosmic celebration has taken place in heaven. God has thrown a huge party because you have been born again into his family—you have been found.

If you haven't accepted Jesus Christ as your Savior, God is waiting. A giant banner has your name on it, the confetti is bagged, and he's ready to throw a party just for you. You matter that much to God. Jesus says in Luke

15:10, "There is rejoicing in the presence of the angels of God over one sinner who repents."

God tells us how much we matter to him in a thousand different ways—throughout the pages of the Bible from Genesis to Revelation. We can either choose to believe the truth based on God's Word, or we can continue believing the lies we've heard in the past about our worth.

Opening up to the truth and relying on what God's Word says is the first step to rebuilding a healthy self-esteem. Receiving and believing the truth about ourselves is the foundation for the next level of the building process that we'll discuss in the following chapter.

CHAPTER 5

HELP!

✳

On a fairly regular basis, during our weekly date nights, Lisa and I will walk into a restaurant and see other church members there. As our church grows, this happens more and more frequently. We'll say, "Hi, how are you doing?" and have a pleasant conversation, then go to our table and sit down.

On occasion, over the course of the meal, Lisa and I will get into an intense "discussion" over some issue. Usually I try to act like everything is cool, that we're not arguing at all. I don't want to appear in a bad light before church members, so I'll say in a forced whisper, "Lisa, we can't talk about this right now. There are people from our

church sitting right over there." I lean my head incon-
spicuously toward their table.

Sound familiar? You know, image control.

We all do it to a certain extent, some more than others. We want to keep our problems private. We want to
maintain a certain image, so we put on a happy face and
ignore the real issues that are eating away at us. People
ask, "How are you doing?" And we respond politely, "Oh,
I'm doing great, just great."

Down deep, though, we're dying. We're kind of like a
shirt I once saw with a silkscreen picture of a dead cow on
it. Below the cow, the caption read, "Really, I'm fine."

I'm not saying we're all dead meat, but we're not all
fine. And the sooner we recognize that, the sooner we can
do the work necessary to rebuild and recover our damaged
self-esteem.

ASKING FOR HELP

Recognizing our problem, though, is just the beginning.
That's the catalyst for change, but real change actually begins when we move to the second step in our three-step
process of rebuilding a damaged self-esteem. It's when we
turn to God and say, "I need help!" For those of us who've
been treadmill hopping, searching for a sense of worth, it's

time at long last to admit that only God can effect real change in our lives.

The first step toward recovering our lost sense of worth is saying, "God, I admit that I need your help and your power to find what I've been searching for all my life." That's a huge step, and most of us just skip over it. We don't stop to admit that without God we're lost on the journey toward a super self-esteem.

The reason many of us have skipped over that crucial step is that we still want to be the boss. Our sinful nature still battles within us. We want to forge our own future, carve our own path. We want to be autonomous, independent. Because of our pride and because we still think we know what's best for us, we want to kick God out of the control center of our lives. In other words, we want to play God.

That's pretty radical rebellion, isn't it? Yet that's exactly

> BECAUSE OF OUR PRIDE AND BECAUSE WE STILL THINK WE KNOW WHAT'S BEST FOR US, WE WANT TO KICK GOD OUT OF THE CONTROL CENTER OF OUR LIVES.

what we do. We can trace the roots of our rebellion all the way back to the Garden of Eden. God knew that a faith that has not been tested cannot be trusted, so he tested Adam and Eve's commitment. He gave them one restriction, one test of faith: do not eat the forbidden fruit.

THE SAD THING IS, IT OFTEN TAKES A CRISIS BEFORE WE'RE WILLING TO DEAL WITH OUR BAGGAGE.

They failed the test.

And from that moment on, we've been messed up. We struggle with the issue of control, trying to be the boss. When we blow the test, the first thing we do is try some image control. We figuratively cover ourselves with fig leaves so God and other people won't notice that we've lost control, we've messed up.

We try so hard to camouflage our pain, but God uses pain as an alarm to wake us up to a problem. Sometimes he lets a crisis or catastrophe occur to spur us to change. The sad thing is, it often takes a crisis before we're willing to deal with our baggage.

I have purchased only one thing in my life from the Home Shopping Network: a triathlon watch. I waited through the allotted shipping days, and sure enough, the item was delivered to my home. But there was a problem with the watch (or maybe with the user). Try as I might, I could not get the alarm to stop going off at odd times. I read the directions and pressed the buttons in every conceivable combination, but I couldn't figure it out.

After a couple of nights of being alarmed out of my sleep, I took the watch, put it in one of my size-12 tennis shoes, stuffed three athletic socks in after it, and piled four towels over the shoe for extra muffling.

I could still hear the annoying beep of the alarm.

People do the same with their pain. They try to cover and camouflage the hurt. They drink to numb it, eat to avoid it, smoke to cloud it, and snort to deaden it. They get angry and criticize others. *If I'm going to be miserable,* they think subconsciously, *I'm going to make sure everyone else is miserable.*

But none of that works. Nothing can completely cover the nagging hurt inside. Only when we admit that we've lost control and ask for help can we resolve the core issues that cause our pain.

Avoid the 4-F Club

Anyone familiar with rural America has likely heard of the 4-H Club. It's an organization that encourages better living through four fundamental tenets related to head, heart, hands, and health. Well, there's another club that doesn't lead to better living. I call it the 4-F Club.

When we fail to admit that we've lost control, when we keep trying to run the show, we end up in the 4-F Club. And it's a club we don't want to join, because it has four fundamental, destructive tenets.

The first tenet is *fear*. When Adam realized he had messed up, with the pulp of the forbidden fruit still on his lips, he hid. Adam was afraid.

If we pretend to be in control and camouflage our pain, we're going to have a lot of fear in this life. Many of us are afraid people might find out who we really are.

We wear masks to cover the fact that deep down inside, our lives are out of control.

The second tenet is *frustration*. David said in Psalm 32:3–4, "There was a time when I wouldn't admit what a sinner I was. But my dishonesty made me miserable and filled my days with frustration" (TLB).

Being unwilling to admit the mess we're in will only leave us frustrated. I think back to times when I've tried to take care of a certain area of my life without God's help. It was a frustrating experience to say the least. After trying without success to be a little demigod, attempting sovereign rule over a universe called Me, I've realized why God is God and I am not.

The third tenet of the 4-F Club is *fatigue*. Living in denial will wear us out. Our strength will evaporate like water on a hot summer day in Texas. Until we finally admit all our sins, all our rebellion toward God, and stop running, we will not find what we're looking for on this journey to the center of our worth. Running away, hiding, covering up our baggage, or jumping from one fun fix to another will exhaust us, because we're not designed to run the show.

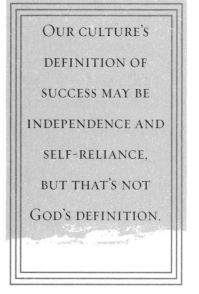

OUR CULTURE'S DEFINITION OF SUCCESS MAY BE INDEPENDENCE AND SELF-RELIANCE, BUT THAT'S NOT GOD'S DEFINITION.

Finally, joining the 4-F Club brings *failure*. Proverbs 28:13 says, "You will never succeed in life if you try to hide your sins. Confess them and give them up; then God will show mercy to you" (GNT). That means we need to articulate our shortcomings: "God, I've messed up. I'm a failure without you."

Our culture's definition of success may be independence and self-reliance, but that's not God's definition. The only way to avoid failure is to confess that God holds all the keys to true success.

Just Ask

Several years ago my family and I were out with some friends in their motorboat when my friend said he'd like to see me water-ski. He had been with me during my first unsuccessful attempt, and he encouraged me to try again.

I don't like to do something I can't do well, but neither do I like to back down from a challenge. So I jumped into the cold water and tried desperately to remember what I was supposed to do. I didn't ask my friend. I thought I could do it without help.

I got on the skis and into the starting position. The boat took off. I fell.

And then I fell again, and again. Finally, when the boat came around after the fifth try, I called out, "I need some help. What am I doing wrong?"

Too many of us are in that same situation when it comes to issues of self-esteem. We think, *I'll put off asking for help until next week or next year. I can control it. I can do it.*

Here's the deal, though. If we had the power to control

it ourselves, we would have already reached our goal. Right?

How long are we going to wait before we admit that we can't do it on our own? It's time to just ask.

When God looks at our lives, he sees all the baggage weighing us down. We think we're ready to board God's flight, but he wants us to stop and let him take our bags. He wants us to ask for help. We can't deal with all that stuff. Isn't it about time we admit that?

CHRIST'S POWER TO HELP

After we've come to a place where we can admit we need help, we need to lay ourselves at the feet of the only person who has the power to help us. We have to believe that Jesus Christ has the power to restore our lost sense of worth. Only Jesus has the power to do it.

Our self-worth actually comes from outside ourselves. Some believe the source is a higher power and even seek that power for help. That's great. But we need to go a step further, to look more closely at that higher power. When we do, we'll see that God has a face, and that face belongs to Jesus.

In Acts 17, when the apostle Paul went to Athens, he

spoke to a bunch of philosophers and armchair theologians who had a concept of a higher power. Paul told them that was good, but they had an underdeveloped picture of who God is. He filled in that picture for them, explaining that the true God is not some man-made being or idea. He is the King of kings and the Lord of lords. He is the same God who sent Jesus Christ to die on the cross for all our sins—and to rise again.

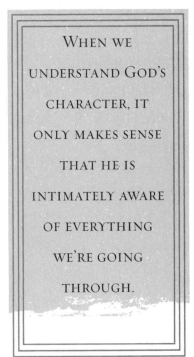

WHEN WE UNDERSTAND GOD'S CHARACTER, IT ONLY MAKES SENSE THAT HE IS INTIMATELY AWARE OF EVERYTHING WE'RE GOING THROUGH.

Paul gave the Athenians a clearer vision of God, and that is precisely the role of the church. It's our job, those of us who have encountered this higher power, to fill in the gaps for others about who he is: Jesus Christ.

Trusting anything else, whether philosophy, science, or another religion, will leave us disappointed and incomplete. The only way to reach our journey's ultimate destination—spiritually, emotionally, and relationally—is to believe that Jesus Christ has the power to heal us and change us.

He Knows

How do we allow Christ to effect real change in our lives? First, we must acknowledge daily that he knows about our problems and our pain. When we understand God's character, it only makes sense that he is intimately aware of everything we're going through.

Some will say, "No one really knows the pain I felt after I lost my father or when my mate left. No one knows how much loneliness or insecurity or fear I feel. No one knows what I'm struggling with."

We can all add two words to those sentences: No one knows . . . *like Jesus.* David was speaking to the Lord when he said, "You keep track of all my sorrows. You have collected all my tears in your bottle. You have recorded each one in your book" (Psalm 56:8 NLT). Tears in a bottle. God has a bottle containing all the tears we have shed in our lives. He has counted them and knows about every one.

Psalm 31:7 says, "You have listened to my troubles and have seen the crisis in my soul" (TLB). I love those words.

We can't hide anything from God. Nothing we do, think, or feel is on the sly. He sees it all.

He Cares

Jesus not only knows about our problems and our pain—he cares. The Bible calls Jesus the Good Shepherd because he is tender and sympathetic to the needs of his flock. Yet he also knows when to employ tough love through discipline. He strikes the perfect balance between correction and compassion.

Consider Jesus's own words: "I am the good shepherd. The good shepherd lays down his life for the sheep. The hired hand is not the shepherd who owns the sheep. So when he sees the wolf coming, he abandons the sheep and runs away. Then the wolf attacks the flock and scatters it. The man runs away because he is a hired hand and cares nothing for the sheep" (John 10:11–13).

I think this is one of the greatest passages in all of Scripture because it spells out Christ's relationship with us. Why does he care so much for us? Because we're his. We belong to him. When Christ purchased our pardon by laying down his life, he pulled us back from the jaws of the Enemy.

No matter what we're going through, no matter how

far we stray from the sheep pen, Christ will not abandon us. Jesus is not some hired hand being paid by the hour. He is the shepherd, the owner of the sheep, and he is always there, loving us, forgiving us, and helping us.

He Can Do It

To break through the pain of our past and reconstruct our self-esteem, we also need to believe that God can change us. And not only that he can change us, but that he wants to.

I like what Ephesians 1:19–20 says: "I pray that you will begin to understand how incredibly great his power is to help those who believe him. It is that same mighty power that raised Christ from the dead and seated him in the place of honor at God's right hand in heaven" (TLB).

The word *believe* in this passage indicates more than intellectual assent; it means to have faith in, to put one's weight on, to trust completely. When we have that kind of faith, we have access to the same power that raised Christ from the dead. That's some awesome power.

God doesn't experience power shortages or failures. His power is there for us. He can change us if we will allow him to.

Accept His Offer

That brings us to the final thing we need to do if we want to change. We must accept God's offer.

God knows about our past, our problems, and our pain. He cares about us deeply. He has the power to change us. And he's offering his help and guidance. But we have to be willing to accept his help.

Here's the great part: God will even give us the ability to ask for help. He gives us the power, the will, and the desire to turn to him for guidance. Philippians 2:13 says, "God is at work within you, helping you want to obey him, and then helping you do what he wants" (TLB).

So we really have no excuses. God gives us the desire to change, and he gives us the power to change. That's an incredible thought. No matter what we're going through, no matter where we are in our journey, it's time to say, "God, by faith I'm ready to make a change. Help me!" And he will do it.

CHAPTER 6

DIVING IN

When my son, EJ, was three years old, I decided it was a good time to teach him to jump off a diving board. He wore little arm floats to keep him from drowning, but he was still skeptical.

"Daddy, catch me. Be right there at the end of the diving board."

"EJ, I'm going to be in the water with you. It'll be over your head, but jump. You can do it."

I watched him walk to the end of the board, curl his toes over the edge, close his eyes, and cover his face.

When he finally got up the nerve to jump, I let him sink a little and then float back to the surface. But I was right there with him. I wasn't going to let him go, because he's my child.

God is waiting for us, his children, to dive into His best for our lives with confidence and assurance. That's the third and final step in rebuilding our self-esteem. Opening up to God's truth and asking him for help are both critical steps, but we also need to move forward into our future with the confidence that God will not abandon us. It's time to take a leap of faith. He's waiting at the end of the diving board, saying, "Go for it. You can do it."

DIVE INTO REPLENISHING RELATIONSHIPS

One of the greatest Bible verses about relationships is this: "Do not be misled: 'Bad company corrupts good character'" (1 Corinthians 15:33). This wisdom applies to all ages at all times. It's as relevant in our lives today as it was when it was written.

If we're serious about repairing our damaged self-esteem, we have to intentionally choose good company. We need to spend time with people who will build us up, not tear us down. There are people out there whose divine mission, whose focus, is to help others rebuild their self-esteem. These people live to reaffirm others because of one simple yet profound fact: they know Jesus Christ.

On the opposite end of the spectrum are those people whose sole mission seems to be to Pac-Man our self-esteem. They're sabotage experts who eat away at our self-esteem the way Pac-Man chomps into Blinky, Pinky, Inky, and Clyde. These people bite into our sense of self-worth with harmful words and piercing looks. Just when we feel like we have a firm foundation and can begin reconstruction, these people come along and gobble it up.

As we go through this process of repairing our self-esteem, let me make two suggestions related to how we choose and maintain relationships.

Limit Your Exposure

The first thing we need to do is limit our exposure to the Pac-Man people in our lives.

Too many of us hear a suggestion like this but don't heed it. We think, *That means I might have to change jobs,* and we balk. But if our self-esteem is being systematically sabotaged at work, then we need to change jobs.

In some cases, our self-esteem saboteurs may be closer than the next cubicle. The harm to our self-esteem may be coming from a friend or even a family member. What do we do when we can't just walk away?

If we want the intensive self-esteem rebuilding process to continue, sometimes it's wise to refrain from visiting that person as often as usual during our reconstruction period. Once we can recognize the lies about our worth and not accept them as reality, then time with that person won't be as harmful, and we can return to more frequent contact.

But what if the Pac-Man in our lives is even closer than a friend or family member? For some, the self-esteem damage is inflicted by a spouse.

In those situations we should go to the person in love and say something like, "When you speak down to me, when you treat me like a possession, or when you disregard my concerns, it diminishes my sense of worth. God tells me that I matter deeply to him, but in order for me to gain the self-esteem God wants me to have, I need you to support and affirm me—not tear down my confidence."

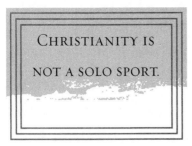

CHRISTIANITY IS NOT A SOLO SPORT.

Often our spouses don't even realize the harm they're doing. They may be acting out of their own insecurities, hurting us because of pain they've experienced in the past. But if we confront them in love and they don't respond in a helpful way, professional marriage counseling may be needed. Working together through these issues with a solid Christian counselor can help build a relationship that is affirming and nurturing for both husband and wife.

Join the Right Huddle

Avoiding destructive people is not enough. We must also develop a team of supporters who will echo words and principles from the Bible, people who reflect the heart and conscience of God. When we meet with these people regularly and hear their words of affirmation, the same kind of words Jesus would say, our self-esteem will begin to grow and improve.

Christianity is not a solo sport. Rebuilding our sense of worth is not a project we can complete on our own; it takes a team effort. For this process to work, we must strategically surround ourselves with people with whom we can have real community. People who love us for who we are, not for the paper crowns we have.

Plenty of times in my life I've thought, *You know, I just don't matter very much.* But because I've joined the right huddle—because I have a team of brothers and sisters who love me and affirm me—God sends them to my rescue in the nick of time. When I need it most, I get a call or an invitation to lunch. I get the message I so desperately need at that time: "Ed, you matter."

Which huddle are you in? Are your relationships tearing you down, corrupting good character? You won't be able to really begin rebuilding your self-esteem until you join a huddle of friends who affirm you and help you through the process.

DIVE INTO BETTER BEHAVIOR

If we're honest with ourselves, we'll admit that our behavior has a lot to do with our self-esteem. Sometimes we look in the mirror and think, *I know that God says I matter. And my friends say I matter, that I'm somebody. But I am acting like a nobody. I'm making mistakes, failing.*

That's when we need to look seriously at our actions and dive into better behavior that leads to better, more confident living. When we sin—when we fall short of the way God wants us to act—not only are we an embarrassment to God, but we're also tearing ourselves apart. We're sabotaging our own self-esteem through our destructive and defiant behavior.

On the other hand, as we move one step at a time toward better behavior, we're gaining the confidence we need to achieve the kind of life God wants for us: a life of obedience to his principles and faith in his goodness. It's a lot like running an obstacle course.

A few years ago, I ran an obstacle course as part of an athletic competition. The course had tires, ropes, tubes to crawl through, and

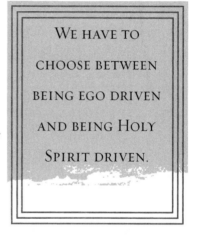

WE HAVE TO CHOOSE BETWEEN BEING EGO DRIVEN AND BEING HOLY SPIRIT DRIVEN.

water to jump over. The starting gun was fired, and I took off. I tripped up a little at each new obstacle, but I kept going.

Each time I made it past one obstacle, my confidence for taking on the next one grew. When I finally crossed the finish line, I felt great satisfaction.

Life's obstacle course is a series of situations in which we have to choose between being ego driven and being Holy Spirit driven. When we choose God's way, we'll feel a sense of accomplishment that comes from obeying the

Spirit's promptings. As we give generously to the work of the local church, take time out of our day to comfort a friend who's down, or say a simple prayer to keep impure thoughts from surfacing in our minds, we are cooperating with and furthering the eternal purposes of God. And that's the best self-esteem boost there is.

As we persevere and clear each moral hurdle, our confidence to overcome the next one will increase. We can say to ourselves, *Yes! I made it past another obstacle!* And our self-esteem will grow.

EVERY TIME WE STRAY, EVERY TIME WE SIN, WE TEAR DOWN OUR SELF-ESTEEM.

But when we hit a section of the course that's difficult, if instead of obeying the leading of the Holy Spirit, we chicken out, we'll damage our self-esteem. If instead of thinking pure thoughts, we think lustful thoughts, we're off course. When we choose to be selfish with our money rather than being sacrificial and generous, we're off course.

Every time we stray, every time we sin, we tear down our self-esteem. So if we're serious about rebuilding our self-esteem, we have to ask ourselves, "How is my behavior affecting the process?"

God wants each of us to live like a somebody, to live a holy lifestyle. We should look at each situation we face, each moral hurdle, as a part of an obstacle course. We should say, "I'm going to get past that one. I'm going to trust God and do it his way!"

DIVE INTO THE CAUSE OF CHRIST

As we continue to work our way through this third step toward rebuilding our self-esteem, we need to consider what we do with the gifts, talents, and abilities God has entrusted to us. To achieve our ultimate self-esteem, to see ourselves the way he sees us, we must dive into the cause of Christ.

Our Vocation

God has empowered us with gifts and abilities. Each of us has unique skills. Some of us are attorneys, construction workers, or doctors. Others are janitors, professional athletes, or homemakers. The list is almost endless. And that's good—that's how life should be. We don't need to concern ourselves with what we cannot do. We just need to focus on what God has given us the ability to do and then do it with all our hearts.

Colossians 3:23–24 says, "Whatever you do, work at it with all your heart, as working for the Lord, not for men, since you know that you will receive an inheritance from the Lord as a reward. It is the Lord Christ you are serving."

What we do is not as important as the level of excellence and commitment with which we do it. We are to live and work in a manner consistent with our value as children of God. When we do this, when we put everything we have into what we do, we live and work the way God intended.

Doesn't it feel good to complete a project that took all the skill we could muster? Don't we get a real self-esteem boost after getting that difficult customer to smile? Or after helping a client find a perfect home? Or after performing flawlessly the surgery that took hours? Or after getting the kids to bed after a full day of caring for home and family? That surge of satisfaction is good; it's a self-esteem boost that will spur on the reconstruction project of your confidence and sense of worth.

Too many of us, though, are living Sealy Posturepedic lives. We're relaxing when we should be working; we're slothful when we should be energetic; we're lazy when we should be moving. And we're missing out on the self-esteem boosts God has laid out for us.

Satan would like nothing better than to keep us in a vocational funk so we end up working halfheartedly. The end result would be wasted potential, missed opportunities, and profound regret.

That's not what God wants. He is beckoning us to the edge of the diving board and prompting us to dive into the fulfilling work he has set before us.

I had a phone conversation recently with a man who was considering leaving his church work and going into another profession. He had received a generous job offer, and his growing family needed the money. He asked me, "Is it wrong for me to leave my position at the church to go into business?" Basically, what he was asking was, does ministry only happen if you work for a church?

Absolutely not!

We work for the Lord wherever we are. God calls each

GOD IS BECKONING US TO THE EDGE OF THE DIVING BOARD AND PROMPTING US TO DIVE INTO THE FULFILLING WORK HE HAS SET BEFORE US.

of us to serve him based on our gifts and abilities. The fact that I work for a church and someone else works for a law firm or a bank or a plumber is not the issue. The issue is, in whatever vocation God has placed us, are we working for him with all our hearts?

Our Mission

Not only has God given us vocations that we are to dive into, he's also assigned each of us a specific mission.

What is your mission in life? Is it just to put more zeros before the decimal point on your paycheck? Is your mission to collect all the toys and trinkets you can? If so, you're missing out on the awesome life God has in store for you, because life is much more than money and material possessions.

Second Corinthians 4:18 helps us get the right perspective on material goods: "What is seen is temporary, but what is unseen is eternal." We need to figuratively put a red tag on every material possession we have and stamp the word *temporary* on it. We need to label our houses, boats, cars, vacation homes, clothes, money, this book . . . everything.

One day we will face God's judgment, and all the stuff

we've acquired will go up in smoke. None of it really matters. None of it will really give us the esteem and confidence we crave, no matter how much we pile up.

Only one thing on this earth is not temporary: people. Each of us is an eternal soul. We will live forever, and our heavenly bank accounts are measured by our impact on the lives of others.

Are we investing our lives in people who matter to God? That's why Christ came. People are at the heart of his mission. Until we dive into something bigger than ourselves—the cause of Christ—our self-esteem will remain deficient. Our full worth will not be realized.

As Christians, if anything stirs us more than the cause of Christ does, something is wrong. That misplaced passion will take us down a path that destroys our self-esteem. We've got to change course and give ourselves to the only pursuit that will restore our proper sense of self-worth: God's mission.

When we commit ourselves to the process of rebuilding our self-esteem—opening up to the truth, asking for help, and diving into God's best for our lives—the transformation will be amazing. We will finally begin to see ourselves the way God sees us.

CHAPTER 7

CONSTRUCTION SIGHT

My sister-in-law and her husband built a beautiful custom home several years ago in Columbia, South Carolina. They documented the entire project with pictures, and after the house was finished, I had a chance to look through the photo album.

The first picture was of their family standing on a wonderful wooded lot with rolling hills. In the foreground was a sign that read "Future Home of Smith and Laurie Parrish." The following pictures showed the various stages of construction: pouring the foundation, building the frame, wiring, and landscaping. The various subcontractors worked diligently, each doing his or her part to complete the house. It was an eye-opening depiction of the work it took to complete that house.

I remember thinking that God must look at human beings like construction projects. We're like undeveloped wooded lots, and he wants to build into our lives a beautiful, structurally sound self-esteem. He accomplishes this task through subcontractors. The Master Builder provides the building materials, the blueprints, and the specs, and then he assigns the necessary work to us.

God uses you and me to build self-esteem in people we encounter. And this one thing is vital to remember: we will never lock eyes with someone who does not matter to God. *Everyone* is important to God.

In order for us to build confidence and a healthy self-respect into the people around us, we must see each of them as an individual construction SIGHT. In this chapter we're going to look at five ways we can build up the self-esteem of others:

> Support *their uniqueness*
> Inspire *them with responsibility*
> Give *criticism carefully*
> Hear *their messages*
> Touch *their hearts*

106

SUPPORT THEIR UNIQUENESS

Let's think for a minute about the people in our lives. Do we really love them for who they are? Do we value their unique impact on our lives?

Jesus showed us how to appreciate and support each person's uniqueness by the way he treated his closest friends. Peter, for example, one of the disciples in Jesus's inner circle, was rash and impulsive at times, but he was also a motivator and a leader. Despite the fact that he denied Christ three times, Jesus forgave him and restored him. Jesus valued Peter's fire and passion so much that he commissioned him to play a pivotal role in the formation of the church.

John, another of Christ's closest disciples, was a sensitive and compassionate man. Because of that, Jesus chose John, "the disciple whom he loved" (John 19:26), to care for his mother after he was gone. John also may have had a keen creative bent that Christ recognized; he was chosen to record the beautifully descriptive prophetic visions found in the book of Revelation.

Despite the differences between these two men, Jesus supported and applauded the uniqueness of each equally. He loved them unconditionally, intentionally, and strategically.

Christ's example translates well into family life, too. Parents who have more than one child are often amazed at how utterly different each child is from the other. Even though they're raised by the same people, in the same manner, in the same house, and with the same disciplinary techniques, the kids are different. Each is unique.

Honest parents will often confess, "The child who's a chip off the old block, the one who's just like I was at that age, is easy to encourage. It's no problem to support him." But the difficulty comes in affirming and building confidence and self-esteem into the child we don't relate to as easily.

But as parents we have a point position, a foreman's job in the construction of our children's self-esteem. We have the God-given power to build them up and launch them into the world armed with stellar self-assurance. And we have the God-given responsibility to support our kids. We need to lay a foundation of a healthy self-esteem by applauding and supporting their uniqueness.

One way we can do that is to support their interests. I've spoken with too many parents who are damaging their children's self-esteem without realizing it by not affirming the unique abilities and interests each child has. The stereotypical example is an athletically inclined father who forces his artistically gifted son to play sports when all the kid wants to do is draw or sing or act.

If we try to live vicariously through our children, either by pushing them to do what we did or to realize our unfulfilled dreams, we're essentially telling them that their gifts, abilities, and aspirations are not important. We're telling them that their worth hinges on whether they follow our dreams.

WE MUST NOT SEND THE MESSAGE THAT THEY NEED TO BE LIKE US IN ORDER TO RECEIVE OUR LOVE.

It's time for some of us as parents to have our cages rattled. We love our children, but do we really demonstrate that love by supporting each child's uniqueness? Do we love them purposefully and intentionally?

The Bible tells us, "Love does not demand its own way" (1 Corinthians 13:5 NLT). Whether we're dealing with children, friends, parents, or the person on the street, we must not send the message that they need to be like us in order to receive our love. God wants us to love and support them in their uniqueness.

With Christ's example as a backdrop, let's look at just a couple of practical ways we can support the unique qualities of the individuals in our lives.

Compliment

When was the last time you complimented a friend, a coworker, a pastor, a brother or sister, or your parents? You know how good it feels when someone says something positive to you, like, "You're so creative," or "You did a great job on that project," or "You have such a great sense of humor." Why not take a moment today to compliment someone. It could make their day or even their entire week. There's no telling the positive impact a sincere compliment can have.

Many people actually push away from relationships because of poor self-esteem. They've had such negative experiences that they're afraid to try again. But here's the great thing. Each of us has the ability to give others a shot of self-esteem with a simple compliment. Every positive word we share gives them renewed confidence.

Verbal affirmation is especially important for parents to give. As we saw in chapter 2, self-esteem is formed early, so we need to start complimenting our kids when they're small. We can start by taking note of what motivates and excites them. If one likes to play musical instruments and march around the house like he's in the band, let's compliment him on his performances. As our children grow, we can compliment them on their science experiments or the play they were in or how kind they are to others or that skillful repair job (even if they created the need for a repair). We need to let them know that their unique abilities are valuable.

Don't Compare

All children are different; all parents are different; each friend and coworker and boss is different. God intentionally created each of us to be different. So we need to avoid making derogatory comparisons. Saying, "Why can't you be more like . . ." to our kids or to an employee—or to ourselves—is rejecting God's creative genius. And it tears down that person's self-esteem rather than building it up.

Let's consider business relationships. Managers can help build self-esteem into the people they're called to lead; or they can blast their employees' confidence to pieces. True, it can be difficult to support a person's uniqueness when he or she does the job differently than you would. It's so easy to make an instant comparison: "Well, that's not the way I would have done that." Because employees are often seen as company assets rather than as relational people, the goal of building their self-esteem is frequently absent.

Too many bosses have the mind-set that their employees are just there to build the bosses up and make them look

LET THEM DO THE JOB ACCORDING TO THEIR SPECIFIC TALENTS AND ABILITIES, AND THEN WATCH THEIR SELF-ESTEEM SOAR.

good. The idea of affirming each person's uniqueness isn't even on their radar screen. And admitting that their subordinates might have a better way of doing things is even further from their minds.

But instead of stifling creativity by demanding cookie-cutter production, we should support the individual ways employees work. Let them do the job according to their specific talents and abilities, and then watch their self-esteem soar. When that happens, not only will they feel better about their work, the business will benefit as well.

What about in marriage? Are we supporting and affirming our spouses' unique gifts? Do we value their contributions? We need to encourage and appreciate each other's differences rather than allowing them to pull us apart.

True, it's easy to say variety is the spice of life, but it's not so easy to live out. Yet by allowing our spouses to be the unique individuals they are, without making unwanted and unnecessary comparisons with ourselves or our ways, we can strengthen their self-esteem and help their confidence to grow. Then we become living representatives of Christ, helping them see themselves the way he sees them.

Inspire Them with Responsibility

The second phase of construction, when we're helping build others' self-esteem, is to inspire them with responsibility.

Responsibility is a self-esteem steroid. When we give someone a responsibility, whether that person is a child, coworker, friend, or spouse, we're communicating trust in that person. And trust is a major catalyst in moving people toward self-confidence.

Proverbs 11:13 says, "You can put confidence in someone who is trustworthy" (GNT). And people can only prove trustworthy by taking on responsibility. At home, it's allowing our kids to borrow the car, to use Dad's tools, to help in the kitchen, or to go to summer camp. In the marketplace, it's letting employees put together the sales presentation without us, run a staff meeting on their own, or write the report for the company president. Among peers, it's trusting someone enough to share our deepest hurts and our greatest hopes.

After graduating from seminary, I went to work in a large church. In fact, it was and still is one of the ten largest churches in America. I remember the first time my boss walked into my office and said, "Ed, we want you to give the opening prayer this Sunday." That may not seem like a huge task. But for me, a twenty-something fledgling pastor, even praying in front of thousands of people was a little intimidating. I can still remember anxiously stepping up to that imposing wooden podium as several thousand eyes locked on to me, waiting for me to speak.

As weak-kneed and nervous as I was, that opportunity gave me a self-esteem boost. By giving me a greater level of responsibility, my supervisor communicated that he trusted me. And I jumped at the chance to display my trustworthiness. My self-esteem as a pastor and public speaker improved exponentially. Now, as I speak every week in front of thousands of people at Fellowship

Church, I can see how God used that simple opening prayer many years ago to give me a jump-start of confidence for the plans he had in store.

Are we doing that for people in our place of employment? Are we inspiring them with responsibility? Or are we hovering, always looking over their shoulders, never trusting them to make a greater personal contribution? That kind of leadership is overprotective, and overprotection is a form of rejection—at work and at home.

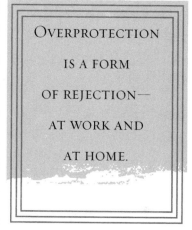

OVERPROTECTION IS A FORM OF REJECTION—AT WORK AND AT HOME.

When I was growing up, a family with three boys lived several houses down from us, and my brother, Ben, and I often played with them after school. We always had to play in their yard, though, because their parents wouldn't let them play anywhere else.

One afternoon we were playing flag football (because they weren't allowed to play tackle). When one of the brothers went back to pass on about the third play of the game, Ben and I went after him to grab his flag. He dodged to miss us, slipped, and fell to the ground, scraping his knee. As we were picking him up and making sure he was OK, his mother came flying out of the house.

"Ed and Ben," she screamed at the top of her lungs, "it's time for you to go home!" Then she yelled to her son, "I've told you to never fall in the grass. Get inside this instant! You could have been killed playing that rough game!"

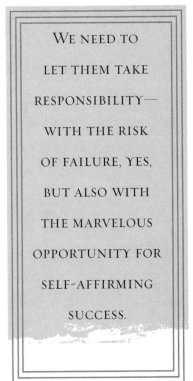

WE NEED TO LET THEM TAKE RESPONSIBILITY— WITH THE RISK OF FAILURE, YES, BUT ALSO WITH THE MARVELOUS OPPORTUNITY FOR SELF-AFFIRMING SUCCESS.

My brother and I could actually see the withering effect of this overprotective mother on our friends. It was like the boys had to scrape what was left of their self-esteem off the turf.

The damage to people's self-esteem from an overbearingly watchful eye can be long-lasting and deep. Instead of smothering others and suffocating their sense of worth, we need to let them take responsibility—with the risk of failure, yes, but also with the marvelous opportunity for self-affirming success.

Jesus was the master at inspiring others this way. In John 20:21, just before he ascended to heaven, Christ gave his disciples this mandate: "As the Father has sent me, I am sending you."

Jesus entrusted the worldwide gospel ministry to a group of ordinary people. He gave them the ball. Imagine their soaring sense of worth as the Son of God handed off this immense responsibility—to them.

Are we trying to do everything on our own? Do we hover over our children or employees or spouses instead of letting them take responsibility? Too often we hold back the confidence and trust that can make a difference in the lives of others and even improve our relationships with them. But when we entrust them with responsibility, we inspire them—and add the next support beam to the frame of their self-esteem.

GIVE CRITICISM CAREFULLY

The third element in self-esteem construction is careful criticism. That may seem strange, but the right manner of criticism can actually build a person's confidence and sense of worth.

I'll never forget the summer I joined about seven

hundred young people on a beach retreat to Padre Island in the Gulf of Mexico. One night I had the opportunity to have a one-on-one conversation with a young man about his life.

As the conversation progressed and hit on the subject of his parents, he began to cry. "Ed, my parents don't love me."

I thought he was kidding. "I know your parents. Of course they love you!"

Then he said something I never thought I would hear from a teenager: "I know they don't, because they let me get away with murder. They don't ever stop me from doing anything."

Discipline is one of the litmus tests of value, and our kids know it. On the surface, they're fighting the rules and restrictions, but inside they're screaming for discipline and careful correction. They want us as parents to confront their character flaws. Sure, they test the limits, always inching their way closer toward the line. But if we don't correct them, if we let them go over the line time and time again, it's devastating to them. When we don't set boundaries, we leave them adrift.

Now, I'm not talking about becoming a disciplinary freak. I'm not saying our homes should be run like Marine

Corps boot camp. But I am talking about setting certain parameters. When our children cross the line, they need to face the consequences. We must discipline and correct them carefully, with love.

When we tell our children they're out of line and correct their behavior, it really does build self-esteem. They will eventually realize, *Whoa, I really must have value for Mom and Dad to take this much time, energy, and effort to keep me in line. I must matter if they don't want me to shipwreck my life.*

WHEN WE DON'T SET BOUNDARIES, WE LEAVE THEM ADRIFT.

Of course, we'll probably never hear that from them. Not once have any of my kids said, "Mom, Dad, thanks so much for grounding me. My self-esteem really needed a boost." My son has never said, "Dad, thanks for the spanking. It was just the jolt of confidence I needed!" It doesn't happen that way.

The Bible says, though, that at some point our children will call us blessed for instilling discipline in their lives. In Proverbs 31, referring to a godly woman who "speaks with wisdom, and faithful instruction" (v. 26), the writer says, "Her children arise and call her blessed" (v. 28). While this specifically addresses a godly mother, the principle applies to both parents.

Giving criticism carefully isn't just for the parent-child relationship. How should we confront character flaws in the workplace? Do we take the attitude that mistakes will not be tolerated, choosing the path of intimidation? Many do. And for a while, that mentality works.

> AT TIMES CRITICISM IS NECESSARY, BUT IT MUST BE DONE CAREFULLY AND IN THE RIGHT SPIRIT—LOVE.

But here's the problem. Over time, seeds of rebellion are sown, and the people we work with (or who work for us) begin to feel like mindless robots. They no longer use their creativity or initiative in their work. They stop thinking for themselves. They become afraid of taking risks and making mistakes, so they do just enough to stay under the radar. Their self-confidence has been destroyed.

I played for a high-school basketball coach in Houston who subscribed to the intimidation method. During practice, he was a great coach—controlled and calm. But when game time came around, he was transformed into a raving maniac. If we made one mistake, missed one shot, or botched one pass, he would yank us out of the game. Then, after he calmed down a little, he'd look down the bench and say, "Are you ready to get in there and play the right way?"

Playing under those conditions was no fun. Motivation was replaced by intimidation. Our confidence on the court was nil. After the first few games, our team even got nervous during warmups. We were wide-eyed and trembling all the time.

Employees, kids, friends, spouses—too often people have that deer-in-the-headlights look from being harshly criticized. Their self-esteem is so low that they're afraid to make any moves on their own.

We can't treat people that way if we have any hope of helping them build a healthy self-esteem. At times criticism is necessary, but it must be done carefully and in the right spirit—love.

Many relationships lose their way because this component is missing. We don't know how to lovingly confront our friends, coworkers, family members, and fellow Christians so that the result is positive growth. And that should always be the goal. We must never criticize for criticism's sake. The only Christlike criticism is that which helps others grow spiritually, relationally, and emotionally.

Consider God's words to us through the apostle Paul: "Do not let any unwholesome talk come out of your mouths, but only what is helpful for building others up according to their needs, that it may benefit those who listen" (Ephesians 4:29).

In 1 Corinthians 13:4 Paul wrote that love "looks for a way of being constructive" (PHILLIPS). Do we? When we confront and offer a gentle critique in love, it will indeed be constructive criticism. We'll be building self-esteem in others.

HEAR THEIR MESSAGES

We all want to be heard. But if everyone is talking, who's doing the listening? Hearing what others have to say is very important in the construction of their self-esteem.

In golf, when a shot ends up in the deep weeds, it's not uncommon for a player to take a mulligan to improve his or her lie—to move the ball to a better position. One of the most frustrating things in a conversation is when one party is only interested in improving his or her conversational lie.

These people will interject comments like, "Yeah, yeah, that's great . . ." But the whole time, their eyes are darting from right to left, searching the room for someone else to talk to.

Then there are the "pounce people." As we're talking to them, they're looking for any little break in our sentence, any breath between words, where they can pounce. They jump into the conversation, and then they dominate.

They don't let others get a word in edgewise. "Yeah, but do you know what happened to me? I did this, and this happened, and I went there and that happened, and then . . . and then . . . and then . . ." They don't really listen to what others have to say.

Both styles communicate that the other person isn't important enough to hold our attention, and that can be damaging to his or her self-esteem.

We need to honestly evaluate our listening skills. Do we watch our friends' body language when we're talking with them? Are we really listening as our spouses recount the events of their day? Are we hearing our coworkers, or are we waiting to pounce at the first available conversational pause? When our teenagers look at us, they shouldn't see a giant Mick Jagger mouth. Instead of always being bombarded with lectures, they should feel genuinely listened to.

The Bible tells us in James 1:19, "Everyone should be quick to listen." If we're going to build self-esteem in others, we've got to listen to them—their words, their ideas, their feelings—all the messages they send.

TOUCH THEIR HEARTS

The University of California in Los Angeles conducted a study concluding that people (women in particular), in order to maintain emotional and physical health, need at least eight to ten meaningful touches a day.[1]

Did you know that each of us has more than five million touch receptors in our skin?[2] There is power in a touch.

But the power of touch goes beyond the physical. Think about what it means to touch people emotionally and spiritually. When we affirm, compliment, and encourage, we touch people's hearts. How wonderful it feels when someone, for no apparent reason, calls just to thank us for being part of the team or group, or leaves us a little note to tell us how much we matter.

I've made it a point throughout my life and ministry to write notes to people, thanking them for something specific they've done or for what they mean to me personally. It doesn't take long to write a note—a few minutes at most. But that small investment can have a tremendous impact, not only in the lives of the people who receive the notes, but in our own lives as well.

That kind of seemingly insignificant gesture can go a long way toward building someone's self-esteem. It's amazing what can happen. As these small gestures add up, we'll begin to notice the person's confidence growing. We'll see the structure of positive self-worth being built into that person's life. And what we do to help, even though it may seem small, is a crucial part of that construction.

God gives each of us the incredible opportunity to help others along the journey to the center of their worth. But to do that effectively, we must look at each person we meet as an individual construction SIGHT. We need to support their uniqueness, inspire them with responsibility, give criticism carefully, hear their messages, and touch their hearts.

> WHEN OUR TEENAGERS LOOK AT US, INSTEAD OF ALWAYS BEING BOMBARDED WITH LECTURES, THEY SHOULD FEEL GENUINELY LISTENED TO.

That's exactly the way Jesus Christ deals with each one of us. And when we have him in our lives, when he is alive and present in our hearts, we are equipped with his tools to help build in others the self-esteem he has created us all to enjoy.

God gives us the mortar and hands us the hammer and nails. He provides everything we need to help others reconstruct their sense of God-given worth. Jesus even laid out the plans: Love others as he loves us. See them as he does. Treat them as he has treated us. When we do that, we'll discover one of the greatest pleasures available to us in this life—helping someone else realize the incredible importance and value he or she has.

Oh, and one more thing. When we help build a beautiful self-esteem in someone else, we'll recover our own sense of worth because we'll be living out God's mission for our lives. That's what it's all about, isn't it? We're not building self-esteem for its own sake; we're doing it in order to build the kingdom, one life at a time.

CHAPTER 8

THE TOP TEN

Top-ten lists are everywhere. A quick Google search will find a plethora of top tens like these: Top Ten Words of 2004; the FBI's Top Ten Most Wanted List; Top Ten Silly Ways of Determining God's Will; the Top Ten Things I Love about *Star Trek*; the Top Ten Web Sites. Some of David Letterman's popular top-ten lists have been compiled into several books. And do I even need to mention the Ten Commandments?

I've been saying all along that a super self-image simply means seeing ourselves the way God sees us, nothing more and nothing less. So I've compiled a top-ten list of truths from Scripture that show us just how much each individual matters to God. When we take each of these ten spiritual realities to heart, they'll help give us the security, confidence, and power to be all we're meant to be in and through Christ.

I O

I AM CREATED

We are God's workmanship, created in
Christ Jesus to do good works.
EPHESIANS 2:10

The word for *workmanship* in the New Testament's original language (Greek) means a "handiwork" or "masterpiece."[1] In the Old Testament, King David said this about God's creative work: "You made us only a little lower than God, and you crowned us with glory and honor" (Psalm 8:5 NLT). In Psalm 139:14 he said, "I praise you because I am fearfully and wonderfully made; your works are wonderful, I know that full well."

Stay with me now, because this is revolutionary. If God is in the masterpiece-painting business, and we are the subject matter of his artistry, that means we are more valuable than the rarest and most prized work of art on this earth. Each person is a masterpiece more precious than a Picasso because we were created by the Great Artist, God himself.

But since we are living, breathing pieces of art, we aren't finished yet. We're masterpieces in the making. Now, here's the best part. God stands in front of the canvas of our lives ready to complete his work. All we have to do is let go of our own feeble attempts to paint a self-portrait, and hand the art supplies back to the Artist.

If we give God the brush, the palette, and the paint, he will turn our lives into masterpieces beautiful beyond description. He'll give us meaning and purpose as we use our unique personalities, talents, and gifts to do great things for him.

The journey to the center of our worth begins with the realization that God gave us life and continues to work in and through us to accomplish his purpose.

9

I Am Chosen

We know that God loves you and
has chosen you to be his own.
1 Thessalonians 1:4 GNT

It feels great to be chosen for something. Whether we're picked for a team or a club or a special group at work, it makes us feel special—wanted and needed.

God has chosen us to be part of his family.

The creator of the universe chose me and chose you. No one is an afterthought. No one gets in on a wild card. God knew each of us before we were born, and he hand-picked each individual to be his own.

Christ has chosen us. The question is, have we chosen Christ to be the most important person in our lives? Sociologists and psychologists tell us that our self-esteem is shaped by what we believe the most important people in our lives think about us. If we make Jesus Christ the most important person, we can't help but have a healthy, balanced, and biblical self-esteem. If Christ is the Lord of our lives, we're on our way to having a self-esteem that is truly redeemed.

8

I AM PROTECTED

Protect me as you would the pupil of your eye.
PSALM 17:8 TLB

Several years ago I bought a really nice pair of sunglasses. I love those glasses because I can run in them, play basketball in them, or fish in them, and they will not come off. They have a special nosepiece that keeps them snugly on my head. I can relax and have fun, knowing that whatever I'm doing, those sunglasses will protect my eyes.

When David spoke the words of Psalm 17:8 to God, he understood that people are very intentional about protecting their eyes. We block them from the sun's harmful rays with hats, visors, and sunglasses. And when an object comes flying toward our faces or someone tries to hit us, our first instinct is to shield our eyes. Our eyes are precious to us.

Just so, we are precious to God. We're the apple of his eye (Zechariah 2:8), and he will protect us from harm. We can trust that our heavenly Father is watching over us today and every day. David's assurance in Psalm 32:7 can be our assurance today: "You are my hiding place; you will protect me from trouble and surround me with songs of deliverance."

7

I AM COMPLETE

You are complete through your union with Christ.
COLOSSIANS 2:10 NLT

Through Christ we have the total package; we have everything. And our completeness, including our self-esteem, comes from our eternally secure relationship with him.

Philippians 1:6 tells us we can be "confident of this,

that he who began a good work in you will carry it on to completion until the day of Christ Jesus."

When Jesus was dying on the cross for our sins, with his last breath, he cried out, "*Tetelestai*"—a Greek term meaning, "It is finished." Jesus was saying, "I have paid the price. The work is complete." And the term *completion* in Philippians 1:6 comes from the same Greek root as *tetelestai*.

Most of us know people who at one time were close to God. They followed the Lord, they were producing spiritual fruit, but now they've drifted off course. Some

WHEN GOD BEGINS A GOOD WORK, IT'S AS GOOD AS ALREADY DONE.

people believe that as a result, God has folded his arms and shunned them. But Scripture says no. When God begins a good work, it's as good as already done. He will finish it. He will complete it. He'll use anything and everything at his disposal to complete the good work he began in us. Through sanctification, the transformation of our minds and hearts, we will be made complete in him.

I don't know about you, but having that confidence

gives me joy. We all have days when we wonder, can God really complete his work in me, in this self-centered sinner's life? The answer is a resounding *yes!* He will not give up on us. God is a finisher. If he began the work in us through Christ, he will complete it.

6

I AM VICTORIOUS

In all these things we have complete
victory through him who loved us!
ROMANS 8:37 GNT

This biblical promise doesn't just mean that we have won—past tense. It means we keep on winning—a continuous, present action. What do we have victory over? "All these things" refers to the list in verse 35: trouble, hardship, persecution, hunger, poverty, danger, and even death. Because of Christ's great love for us, nothing can defeat us. When he's on our side, we are always on the winning team.

The apostle Paul concluded this portion of his letter with resounding confidence: "I am certain that nothing can separate us from his love: neither death nor life, neither angels nor other heavenly rulers or powers, neither the present nor the future, neither the world above nor the world below—there is nothing in all creation that will ever be able to separate us from the love of God which is ours through Christ Jesus our Lord" (Romans 8:38–39 GNT).

Through the death and resurrection of Christ, we have victory over everything, and our self-confidence should be anchored in that victory. Not even the feeling of winning back-to-back Super Bowls could come close to the incredible victory we have through life in Christ.

5

I Am Saved

He saved us and called us to be his own people,
not because of what we have done, but
because of his own purpose and grace.
2 Timothy 1:9 GNT

The meaning of being saved is usually put in futuristic terms. "I'm saved, so I've got a ticket to heaven. I'm in the club, and I'll be spared from the wrath to come."

Being saved does have implications for the future, and we'll get to those shortly. But salvation also relates to the past and to the present.

How does salvation affect the past? By receiving Christ, we break the penalty of sin. In others words, we don't have to worry about the skeletons in our closets rearing their ugly heads. We no longer have to worry about all the foul-ups accrued over the last year or five years or twenty-five years. Once we're saved, the past is past.

The present reality is that we're saved from the power of sin day by day. As we walk with the Lord, temptation has less of a pull on us. We don't fall into the same old traps Satan puts in our path.

And in the future, we'll be saved from all presence of sin. One day, in the twinkling of an eye, those of us who have entered into a saving relationship with Christ will leave sin behind us forever. When we move from this life to the next, we will spend eternity with the Lord away from the existence of sin.

That's what it means to be saved.

Our self-esteem should skyrocket when we really understand that God has saved us even though we fall short of his perfect standard. If God would go to such lengths as sending his own Son to die for us when we certainly didn't deserve that sacrifice—surely then we can see that we must have incredible worth in his eyes.

4

I AM FORGIVEN

*"I—yes, I alone—am the one who blots out your sins
for my own sake and will never think of them again."*
ISAIAH 43:25 NLT

Many of us think that when something bad happens in our
lives, God is getting even with us for something we did
wrong.

Not true.

Yes, there are consequences to our actions, but God is
not a cosmic kill-joy waiting to hit us over the head for
every mistake. Romans 8:1 says, "There is no condemna-
tion for those who belong to Christ Jesus" (NLT). In other
words, what's done is done; God forgives and forgets.

But can God really forget anything? When God forgives us, he doesn't forget what we've done. Rather, he
chooses not to remember, or rehearse in his mind, our re-
bellious actions. He makes a decision to "never think of
them again."

In the New Testament, the Greek word most com-
monly translated "forgiveness" means to release, to hurl

away, to free one's self. Only that kind of forgiveness—God's perfect forgiveness—can halt the cycle of blame and pain and break the chains that bind us to our past.

When Christ died on the cross for our sins, the Father knew how many times we would blow it. Still he chose to do the work of forgiveness. In his mercy he gave us not what we deserve—death—but rather what we don't deserve—life.

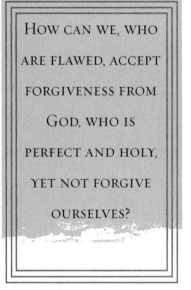

HOW CAN WE, WHO ARE FLAWED, ACCEPT FORGIVENESS FROM GOD, WHO IS PERFECT AND HOLY, YET NOT FORGIVE OURSELVES?

Sadly, many people are not experiencing the abundant life Christ came to offer. Some may have accepted God's forgiveness, even received the gift of eternal life. But they're not *experiencing* God's forgiveness because they haven't forgiven themselves.

How can we, who are flawed, accept forgiveness from God, who is perfect and holy, yet not forgive ourselves? If God has cast our sin as far as the east is from the west (Psalm 103:12), why do we insist on rehearsing our failures? Forgiveness allows us to unchain ourselves from the past. It moves us beyond anger, beyond pain, beyond the insecurities that dog us.

We can take comfort—and confidence—in knowing that our loving and transcendent God has forgiven our sins.

We can forgive ourselves.

And move on.

3

I AM FREE

"You will know the truth, and
the truth will set you free."
JOHN 8:32

I'd venture to say that many of us have never really thought about the implications of that verse. We hear the words, but we don't understand the impact they can have on our lives. God isn't just talking about obtaining intellectual knowledge. Too many of us think knowledge is enough. We also need application.

Having giant study Bibles filled with notes and highlights doesn't make us spiritual giants. Attending every Bible class offered and knowing everything about eschatology, soteriology, hamartiology, Christology, and all the other -ologies won't automatically bring us the freedom of living in the Spirit.

Knowledge is important, but we have to live out that knowledge. And through a relationship with the Truth, we are free to live it out. We can apply that knowledge in a meaningful way in our everyday lives. We're able to go beyond religion, beyond law, beyond have to, into a new way of living.

YOU SEE, TRUTH IS NOT A SET OF FACTS; TRUTH IS A PERSON.

You see, Truth is not a set of facts; Truth is a person. Christ said that he is the Truth (John 14:6). And as we grow in our relationship with the Way, the Truth, and the Life, we stop being chained to our harmful habits and enslaved to our sins.

We are free! Free to pursue a better way. Spiritual freedom is not just being released *from* something; it's also being released *to* something. We are free from sin and free to pursue abundant life.

What better foundation could there be for rebuilding our self-esteem than the freedom from everything that holds us down and toward everything that lifts us up?

Some time ago I stood outside an old courthouse in a small Texas town. The building also housed the county jail, so I could see prisoners peering out the windows at me. They actually were wearing the old-fashioned, black-and-white striped uniforms.

These men and women were incarcerated. In a sense, chained up. But one day they will be set free. How crazy it would seem if, on their liberation day, they chose not to leave the jail—if they said, "I like being incarcerated. It's comfortable—it's what I know. I'm staying right here."

Yet many of us do just that.

Even after accepting Christ's gift of salvation, we stay in a prison cell of poor self-esteem. We have established a personal relationship with Christ, the Truth. We're increasing our knowledge base as we engage in both corporate and personal Bible study. But there's still a problem. We aren't putting into practice what we know. We've been released from the darkness of our prison cell but have not yet stepped into the light of freedom.

We aren't living out the life-changing application, experiencing the abundant life Christ came to give. If we want to live by "the perfect law that gives freedom" (James 1:25), we must first "do what it says" (James 1:22).

Jesus valued us enough to pay for our release with his blood, so isn't it about time to leave the jailhouse and start living like the free people we are?

2

I AM LOVED

"I have loved you with an everlasting love;
I have drawn you with loving-kindness."
JEREMIAH 31:3

Notice that there are no conditions tied to that verse. God's love has no prerequisites.

Many of us grew up thinking that in order to earn the love of others, we had to meet certain conditions—make straight As, score the most touchdowns, or whatever. But God doesn't place any conditions on his love for us. So when we wake up in the morning, we don't have to wonder, *Does God love me today? Have I been good enough?* The Bible tells us that he has drawn us to himself out of loving-kindness.

It's not about what we can do. It's not about how good we can be or how well we perform in front of everybody. It's about who we are in God's eyes and who we can become through the one who loves us perfectly.

When we're loved perfectly, everything else is OK. So as we walk through life—our careers, our relationships, our hopes and dreams—all we need to remember is to sit back and allow God's love to be our all in all.

How do we do that? How do we live in the love of God?

Surrender. We've got to lay down our expectations and desires and let the love of God fill that hole in us that only he can fill.

1

I AM ACCEPTED

Accept one another, then, just as Christ accepted
you, in order to bring praise to God.
ROMANS 15:7

Those of us who are Christians have accepted Jesus Christ. But do we realize that Jesus Christ has accepted us?

Many of us don't think about the reciprocal nature of our salvation. We are accepted by God himself. Knowing this should be reason enough for us to forget the lies that others tell us about our worth. Yet we try to find acceptance in other ways. Remember the treadmills of style, status, and success?

We mistakenly think power, prestige, and pleasure will quench our thirst for acceptance and end our search for significance. Or we try to find self-esteem in relationships. We meet someone and are so excited because we think he or she will meet all our needs. But after a while, we realize this relationship doesn't meet our expectations either.

No matter which treadmill we try, we're not satisfied. Something's still missing, so we move on to the next thing. And if that doesn't work, something else. And so on and so on.

We've got to come to terms with who we are before God. Then and only then will we find true significance.

To help us remember what God thinks about us, we all should write down two things beside Romans 15:7 in our Bible margin:

1. *God thinks about me every second of every day.* He really does. From the moment he made each individual, he's been thinking about us.

2. *I'm so valuable to God that he redeemed me at the cost of his own Son.* We've already discussed the incredible price Christ paid for us. He took the death journey to the cross so we could take this life journey to the center of our worth.

145

The symbol of the cross should always remind us that we are accepted.

Once we understand and embrace the truths on this top-ten list, all the things that have weighed us down, all the stuff that has held us back will begin to fall away. We'll finally be able to see who we are—and help others see who they are—in God's eyes.

As we conclude this book, I have to ask: where are you on the journey to the center of your worth?

From the very beginning, God's desire has been for us to see ourselves the way he does. No, the path toward a super self-esteem is not easy. It's filled with potholes from past mistakes, painful scars, and searing memories. But the destination is well worth the hurts, hurdles, and hardships we encounter along the way.

Don't miss out on all God wants you to be. If you haven't begun, begin. If you're in the middle, persevere. If you're nearing the end, get ready to celebrate. The pain is temporary. But the joy is forever.

NOTES

CHAPTER 1: ME, MYSELF, AND WHY

1. Gary Smith, *Beyond the Game* (New York: Grove Press, 2001), 25.

CHAPTER 7: CONSTRUCTION SIGHT

1. "What Makes Love Last," *Ladies' Home Journal*, http://www.lhj.com/lhj/story.jhtml?storyid=/templatedata/lhj/story/data/14115.xml.

2. "Massage Therapy," Alternative Medicine Therapies, http://library.thinkquest.org/24206/massage-therapy.html?tqskip1=1.

CHAPTER 8: THE TOP TEN

1. Earl D. Radmacher, Ronald B. Allen, and H. Wayne House, eds., *Nelson's New Illustrated Bible Commentary* (Nashville: Thomas Nelson Publishers, 1999), 1534.

STUDY/DISCUSSION GUIDE

by Steve Halliday

This brief discussion guide has been prepared to help you get the most out of *You! The Journey to the Center of Your Worth*. In the first part of each study, "A Journey Back," we'll review some of the most crucial concepts in each chapter and ponder how they impact each of us. In the second part, "A Journey Up," we'll look into what the Bible has to say about the topic under review in order to see how we can build God's best into our lives.

STUDY/DISCUSSION GUIDE

CHAPTER 1
Me, Myself, and Why

A Journey Back

1. Many of us are on a self-esteem treadmill, and we're determined to stay on it even though we seem to be going nowhere fast.

   A. Do you ever feel like you're on a "self-esteem treadmill"? Explain.

   B. When did you last feel as though you were "going nowhere fast"?

   C. What do you do to get off the self-esteem treadmill? How would you help someone else to get off of it?

2. Our journey almost always begins with a five-word question

for which we each desperately want an answer: do I matter to anyone?

    A. Does this five-word question ever bother you? Explain.

    B. When you ask this question, what kind of answers do you usually get?

    C. How do people often ask this question without using these exact words?

3. As long as we search for the answer outside of God and by relying on ourselves, we will never truly satisfy our hunger for self-worth.

    A. Do you agree with this statement? Why or why not?

    B. What does God have to do with your own feeling of self-worth?

    C. When does your hunger for self-worth feel most satisfied?

4. With his lips barely moving, the words seemed to come from the back of the champ's throat: "I had the world and it wasn't nothin'."

    A. What do you think the champ meant?

    B. Have you ever felt anything like this? Explain.

    C. Why do the things that we think will satisfy us often fail to do so?

A Journey Up

1. Read Jeremiah 9:23–24.

    A. What things does God advise us to avoid?

B. What things does God advise us to do? Why?

2. Read Mark 8:36–37.

 A. How would you answer Jesus's question in verse 36?

 B. How would you answer Jesus's question in verse 37?

 C. What course of action should you pursue based on your answers?

CHAPTER 2
Tread-Militant

A Journey Back

1. We tell ourselves, *Yeah, I may be exhausted, but I'm not giving up. I'm going to stick with it, even though I may not be getting anywhere right now. Surely it'll pay off in the long run; I'll gain self-esteem if I just hang in there.*

 A. Have you ever told yourself anything like this? If so, what happened?

 B. Why do we think we'll get a different result if we keep doing the same thing?

 C. Does gaining self-esteem ever exhaust you? Explain.

2. Each of us is a masterpiece. We are living, breathing pieces of art.

 A. Do you *feel* like a masterpiece? Do you *feel* like a stunning piece of art? Explain.

 B. Do you ever keep God's masterpiece hidden away from the eyes of the world? If so, why?

 C. How can you proudly display your life as God's special

creation, without getting a big head or calling attention to yourself?

3. By paying the price—dying for us—at the cross, Jesus regained for us all we had lost as a result of our sin. With his atoning sacrifice, he signed God's masterpiece—God's redemptive painting.

   A. How did Jesus regain for us all we had lost as a result of our sin? How does his work benefit us?

   B. What is an "atoning sacrifice"? Why is one necessary?

   C. Do you think God has "signed" your masterpiece? Explain.

4. Right now, by his grace and by his power, he is saying to us, "Give me your art supplies. I want to do the painting. I'm the artist. I can take your inadequate attempt at finger-painting and make the canvas of your life into something breathtakingly beautiful."

   A. Have you ever given God your "art supplies"? Explain.

   B. How do you think God could make your life into "something breathtakingly beautiful"?

   C. How has God already shown you his artistry by the way he works in your life?

A Journey Up

1. Read Psalm 8:3–8.

   A. What is your place in the universe, according to this passage?

   B. What does God think of you, according to this passage?

2. Read 1 Peter 1:18–19.

    A. What price did God pay to secure your eternal welfare?

    B. How have you responded to his generosity?

CHAPTER 3
Damage Assessment

A Journey Back

1. As harmful as firearms can be to our physical bodies, the words fired at us by others can have a spiritual and emotional effect more devastating than bullets.

    A. Why can words hurt us more than bullets?

    B. What kind of words have devastated you?

    C. If you could wipe out any single conversation you've ever had, what would it be?

2. First we hear the lies others tell us—that we're not good enough, that we'll never make it. We hear damaging words that chip away at our self-esteem. Once those lies infiltrate our minds and hearts, we start to tell ourselves the very same things.

    A. What kind of lies do you tend to tell yourself?

    B. How have these lies hurt you or kept you down?

    C. How can you begin to stop telling yourself these lies?

3. The bottom line is this: whether we do it to get down on ourselves or to set ourselves up on a pedestal, it's unfair to compare. And it's always a losing game.

A. Do you tend more to get down on yourself, or set yourself up on a pedestal? Explain.

B. Why is the comparison game always a losing proposition?

C. How can you get yourself to stop playing the comparison game?

4. Negative criticism is just an attempt to cover the festering wounds in our own self-esteem. It also makes a mockery of God's creative genius.

A. In what way does negative criticism try to cover for our own lack of self-esteem?

B. Why does negative criticism make a mockery of God's creative genius?

C. Have you asked God to inspect your baggage and help you assess the damage? If so, what did you discover? If not, why not?

A Journey Up

1. Read James 3:5–10.

A. What is the main problem with the human tongue?

B. How can we best respond to this problem?

2. Read Ephesians 4:29–32.

A. What things does this passage prohibit?

B. What things does this passage encourage?

C. To what degree is this passage currently lived out in your own life?

CHAPTER 4
Opening Up

A Journey Back

1. Our search for self-esteem is, in reality, a quest to reclaim a real and lasting crown of honor and dignity. We're in constant search-and-rescue mode.

   A. How is a search for self-esteem a "quest to reclaim a real and lasting crown"?

   B. When have you most felt personal honor and worth?

   C. How are you searching to recover lost self-esteem?

2. The first step in rebuilding our self-esteem, in uncovering God's supreme, tailor-made crown for each of us, is opening up to him and allowing him to speak truth into our lives.

   A. How do you most effectively "open up" to God?

   B. What do you think it means for God to "speak truth" into your life?

   C. Have you taken this first step toward rebuilding your self-esteem? If so, when? If not, why not?

3. We need to close the fictional books we've been relying on for our self-worth and turn to the book of reality: the Bible.

   A. What "fictional books" have you relied on for your self-worth?

   B. What results did you get with these "fictional books"?

   C. What kind of results has the Bible given you?

4. God tells us how much we matter to him in a thousand ways—from Genesis to Revelation. We can either choose to believe the truth based on God's Word, or we can continue believing the lies we've heard about our worth.

    A. What lies have you heard about your own worth?

    B. What truths from the Bible have most impacted your own self-esteem?

    C. How can you increasingly rely on and receive strength from the Bible?

A Journey Up

1. Read Luke 15:1–32.

    A. Which of the three stories most resonates with you? Why?

    B. What is the main point in each of the stories?

2. Read Isaiah 43:7.

    A. Why did God make us, according to this verse? What difference does this make?

    B. Who created you? What difference does this make?

CHAPTER 5
Help!

A Journey Back

1. We want to maintain a certain image, so we put on a happy face and ignore the real issues that are eating away at us.

People ask, "How are you doing?" And we respond politely, "Oh, I'm doing great, just great."

A. Why do you think we put on these happy faces?

B. What happens when we ignore the real issues eating away at us?

C. What did you say the last time someone asked you, "How are you doing?"

2. The first step toward recovering our lost sense of worth is saying, "God, I admit that I need your help and your power to find what I've been searching for all my life."

A. How do we know God will help us find what we've been searching for? What guarantees do we have?

B. Why does God insist that we ask him for his help?

C. Have you taken this step? If so, how? If not, why not?

3. After we can admit we need help, we need to lay ourselves at the feet of the only person who has the power to help us. We have to believe that Jesus Christ has the power to restore our lost sense of worth. Only Jesus has the power to do it.

A. Why should we believe that only Jesus has the power to restore our lost sense of worth?

B. Do you believe that only Jesus has the power to restore a lost sense of worth? Explain.

C. How might Jesus go about restoring a lost sense of worth?

4. God knows about our past, our problems, and our pain. He cares about us deeply. He has the power to change us. And he's offering his help and guidance. But we have to be willing to accept his help.

   A. Does it comfort you or worry you that God knows about your past? Explain.

   B. Do you believe that God cares about you deeply? Explain.

   C. Have you been willing to accept God's help? Explain.

A Journey Up

1. Read Psalm 32:3–7.

   A. What difficulties was the writer having? What caused these difficulties?

   B. How did the writer address his problem? What was the result?

2. Read Jeremiah 17:5–8.

   A. How does God react to those who put their trust in mere humans? What happens to them?

   B. How does God react to those who put their trust in him? What happens to them?

CHAPTER 6
Diving In

A Journey Back

1. If we're serious about repairing our damaged self-esteem, we have to intentionally choose good company. We need to

spend time with people who will build us up, not tear us down.

A. Who is the most positive person you know? How much time do you get to spend with this person?

B. Do you intentionally choose "good company" most of the time, or is it more hit-or-miss?

C. Which "huddle" are you in? Are your relationships tearing you down and corrupting good character, or building you up? Are you satisfied with your "huddle," or would you like a change? Explain.

2. We need to look seriously at our actions and dive into better behavior that leads to better, more confident living.

A. Why does better behavior lead to more confident living?

B. Would you say that your behavior tends to lead to confident living? Explain.

C. When did you last take a serious look at your habits? Is it time for a review? Explain.

3. Life's obstacle course is a series of situations in which we have to choose between being ego driven and being Holy Spirit driven.

A. What does it mean to be "ego driven"?

B. How does one become "Holy Spirit driven"?

C. What signs or indications let you know that you're being ego driven rather than Holy Spirit driven?

4. As Christians, if anything stirs us more than the cause of

Christ does, something is wrong. That misplaced passion will take us down a path that destroys our self-esteem.

A. In what way(s) does the "cause of Christ" stir you?

B. How has any misplaced passion damaged your own self-esteem?

C. What is your mission in life?

A Journey Up

1. Read 1 Corinthians 15:33–34.

   A. What general principle is given in verse 33?

   B. What directive is given in verse 34? What rebuke is given? What is the connection between verses 33 and 34?

2. Read Philippians 3:4–11.

   A. What things did the writer once consider of supreme importance? (vv. 4–6).

   B. What things did the writer come to consider of supreme importance? (vv. 7–11). What accounts for this change of perspective?

CHAPTER 7
Construction SIGHT

A Journey Back

1. Whether we're dealing with children, friends, parents, or the person on the street, we must not send the message that they need to be like us in order to receive our love. God

wants us to love and support them in their uniqueness.

    A. How easy is it for you to compliment others? What kind of compliments do you usually give?

    B. Why is it so damaging to make comparisons between different people?

    C. Who in your life most needs you to affirm their uniqueness?

2. Responsibility is a self-esteem steroid. When we give someone a responsibility, whether that person is a child, coworker, friend, or spouse, we're communicating trust in that person. And trust is a major catalyst in moving people toward self-confidence.

    A. Is it easy for you to give responsibility to others? Explain.

    B. Why is trust "a major catalyst in moving people toward self-confidence"?

    C. When you give responsibility to someone, do you often take it back? If so, why? If not, what do you do if the person "messes up"?

3. The right manner of criticism can actually build a person's confidence and sense of worth.

    A. Give several examples of "the right manner of criticism."

    B. How does constructive criticism build someone's confidence and sense of worth?

    C. Does your criticism tend toward the negative or the constructive side? How can you improve the kind of criticism you give?

4. We all want to be heard. But if everyone is talking, who's doing the listening? Hearing what others have to say is very important in the construction of their self-esteem.

   A. Do you tend to talk more or listen more? Explain.

   B. How do you feel when you speak and the person to whom you're speaking is clearly not listening? Why do you feel this way?

   C. How can you make yourself into a better listener? What can you do today to improve?

5. When we affirm, compliment, and encourage, we touch people's hearts. How wonderful it feels when someone, for no apparent reason, calls just to thank us for being part of the team or group, or leaves us a little note to tell us how much we matter.

   A. Describe a time when you got an unexpected compliment or received a kind thank-you note.

   B. What kind of gesture tends to most touch your own heart?

   C. Who in your own life most needs a warm touch from you today?

A Journey Up

1. Read Ephesians 2:10. How does this verse proclaim the priceless and unique value of each one of us?

2. Read John 20:21. What enormous responsibility did Jesus give to his disciples?

3. Read Galatians 6:1. How does this verse counsel us to give criticism and correction?

4. Read James 1:19. What does it mean to be "quick to listen"? Why should we be "slow to speak"?

5. Read 1 Thessalonians 2:7. What is the writer trying to convey to his readers by his use of this unexpected image?

CHAPTER 8
The Top Ten

A Journey Back

Review the following top-ten list:

10   I am created.

9   I am chosen.

8   I am protected.

7   I am complete.

6   I am victorious.

5   I am saved.

4   I am forgiven.

3   I am free.

2   I am loved.

1   I am accepted.

A. How does each statement make you feel?

B. Choose one or two of the statements and meditate on it (them) for a whole day. How does this exercise change your outlook?

C. Which of these truths impacts you the most? Why?

D. Which of these truths do you have the most trouble grasping for yourself? Why?

E. How can you help others to lay hold of these truths for themselves?

A Journey Up

1. Read Psalm 139:14. What perspective does this verse give on your own creation?

2. Read 1 Thessalonians 1:4. For what did God choose you?

3. Read Psalm 32:7. What pictures does the writer use to describe God?

4. Read Colossians 2:10. What does your connection to Christ do for you?

5. Read Romans 8:37. What kind of victory belongs to God's children? How do current circumstances affect this victory?

6. Read 2 Timothy 1:9. From what were you saved? To what are you saved?

7. Read Colossians 2:13–15. What is involved in your forgiveness? What is included in it?

8. Read John 8:36. What kind of freedom does Jesus give you?

9. Read John 16:27. What is God's attitude toward you? Why?

10. Read Romans 15:7. What is Christ's attitude toward you? How are you to respond? What is the result?

Ed Young is a pastor, author, and speaker with a passion for communicating God's unchanging truth through culturally compelling and creative teaching. He is the founding and senior pastor of Fellowship Church, one of the ten largest churches in America. Located in the heart of Dallas/Fort Worth, Texas, the church's main campus sits on 141 acres just north of DFW Airport. The church also operates three satellite campuses—one just north of downtown Dallas, one in the northern suburb of Plano, and one north of Fort Worth.

Each year Fellowship Church (fellowshipchurch.com) hosts the Creative Church Conference (C3). The church also provides ministry tools and resources through creativepastors.com and Fellowship Connection, a network of local churches with a passion for creatively connecting the transforming message of Jesus Christ with this generation. Ed Young Ministries (edyoung.org) airs a weekday radio broadcast in major cities throughout the U.S. and a weekly televised program on several networks, including USA and Daystar.

Ed and his wife, Lisa, have four children and speak often about the importance of following God's agenda for the family. Ed's book *High Definition Living* was written to help Christ followers, regardless of who or where they are, excel as leaders of others for God's glory. His book *Kid CEO: How to Keep Your Kids from Running Your Life* was born out of his desire to help parents exercise their God-given leadership in the home. Ed's other books include *Know Fear, Fatal Distractions*, and a book for church leaders entitled *Can We Do That? 24 Innovative Practices That Will Change the Way You Do Church.* Ed and Lisa are also strong advocates of maintaining an active and healthy lifestyle. And to help people honor the bodies God has entrusted to us, they have produced a series of resources called *Body for God.*

If you enjoy the writings of
Ed Young,
be sure to check out these other great titles

Can We Do That?
(Cowritten with Andy Stanley)
A dynamic tool for today's ministry, this book offers twenty-four exciting practices to help your church communicate Christ to the world—without compromising who and what God has called you to be. Learn things like how to partner with current church attendees to reach the unchurched, how to create a place where kids can take their parents to learn, how to provide real community through small groups, and much more.

ISBN 1-58229-457-7
206 pp • Softcover

High Definition Living
This award-winning book illustrates how anyone can become an effective leader by taking a hard look at one effective biblical leader: Nehemiah. Young uses practical application to demonstrate how Nehemiah led with a consistent, faithful approach while taking a stand for God among naysayers. Learn to intentionally implement the qualities of creativity, enthusiasm, and organization and discover the leader within.

ISBN 1-58229-290-6
224 pp • Hardcover

Available where good books are sold.